Surviving
a Layoff

Surviving a Layoff

A Week-by-Week Guide to Getting Your Life Back Together

LITA EPSTEIN, MBA

Avon, Massachusetts

Published by
Adams Business, an imprint of Adams Media,
a division of F+W Media, Inc.
57 Littlefield Street, Avon, MA 02322. U.S.A.
www.adamsmedia.com

ISBN 10: 1-60550-096-8
ISBN 13: 978-1-60550-096-6

Printed in Canada.

J I H G F E D C B A

Library of Congress Cataloging-in-Publication Data
is available from the publisher.

This publication is designed to provide accurate and authoritative information with regard to the subject matter covered. It is sold with the understanding that the publisher is not engaged in rendering legal, accounting, or other professional advice. If legal advice or other expert assistance is required, the services of a competent professional person should be sought.

—From a *Declaration of Principles* jointly adopted by a Committee of the American Bar Association and a Committee of Publishers and Associations

Many of the designations used by manufacturers and sellers to distinguish their product are claimed as trademarks. Where those designations appear in this book and Adams Media was aware of a trademark claim, the designations have been printed with initial capital letters.

This book is available at quantity discounts for bulk purchases.
For information, please call 1-800-289-0963.

Dedication

This book is dedicated to my husband, HG Wolpin, who supports all my work, as well as puts up with all my idiosyncrasies as I rush to meet writing deadlines.

Acknowledgments

First I want to thank Peter Archer at Adams Media for his support of my work and for giving me the opportunity to do this book. I also want to thank the editorial staff at Adams Media for their work in getting this book ready for publication, including Wendy Simard and Casey Ebert. Finally, I want to thank my agent Jessica Faust, who's helped me over the years to succeed as an author.

Contents

Introduction

We all need to accept the fact that being laid off is just a part of the lifestyle in the United States. Most people will be laid off at least once in their lifetime and many will be laid off multiple times. In my circle of family and friends almost all of the people I know have been laid off at least once unless they work for their state or hold a federal job. And even those people are not as secure as they used to be as local and state government agencies face significant budget cuts. I do know one person, my brother, who has worked in the same company since getting his B.S. in engineering, but that is more the exception than the rule.

At the time of writing this book, the U.S. Department of Labor announced that mass layoffs in June 2008 were the highest since 2003 with 165,697 workers laid off that month. The numbers can be expected to rise. Unemployment was at 5.5 percent, but that doesn't represent true levels of unemployment as many people must take jobs at a much lower salary than they had been earning in their previous job just to put food on the table. Others take part-time jobs, and yet others just give up looking for work completely. Some estimate the jobless rate in this country is closer to 10 percent if one considers the under-employed and those who have given up looking.

You may be wondering what the point is in reviewing all of this bad news. If you're recently laid off, I simply want to assure you that you are not alone. You're part of what is becoming the norm for the U.S. labor market, so don't think you've done anything wrong. Just take some time to heal from the wound of losing your job and then get back in the saddle and look for a new job—once you've taken the time to figure out what that new job should be.

In this book we'll sort through the loss and then help you sort out what you should consider doing next. Don't start looking for your next job right away. Take some time to think about what you want to do and where you want to live. Take time to work through the anger and loss of being laid off before you start looking.

Some people make the mistake of jumping into a job search too soon. If you do so, that will only hurt your chances of finding the right job for you—or finding any job at all. You have to work on yourself before you can start looking to find a new job.

I know. I'm talking from the experiences of surviving three layoffs in my lifetime. As I look back over my career, I realize the layoffs presented opportunities for me to look at what I'd been doing and figure out my next steps. Layoffs didn't hurt my career; instead, they helped me to focus it in new and better directions that ultimately helped me to get to the point where I am today—doing what I love to do.

My first layoff happened after I worked for a couple of years at a university center that was on soft funding—in other words, a foundation grant. When the grant was about halfway through, the center applied for new funding and was unsuccessful in winning an additional grant. Staff was cut and since my salary was fully funded by the grant that was ending, I was let go.

I knew the layoff was likely and once we got the rejection from the foundation I knew I was out the door. But I was young and foolish and didn't do anything to set myself up for my next position. I learned the hard way to always be thinking about what I want to do next. I learned to carefully build a network of contacts and keep that information at home. I learned to keep copies of my successful projects at home so I could easily reference them or present them during an interview.

Unfortunately, these are the mistakes many people make. We're encouraged to be loyal to the company we work for, but can't expect the same loyalty from that company. If the top executives need to improve the company's profit margin, they must focus on the bottom line; and not on the lives of the people they plan to lay off. Too often you hear of companies laying off employees while large bonuses or raises are voted in by the Board of Directors for the top executives. Often a manager is rewarded if they can reduce head count, cut costs, and still get the job done. The people left behind are usually overworked and, with new overtime rules, forced to work longer hours without extra pay.

Loyalty toward a company today is dead. Yes, you should do a good job, but always keep your eye on yourself and what's best for your career.

By the time I got to my third career layoff I had done my homework and felt prepared for the blow. I was working for a dot-com. We'd celebrated a successful month. Staff was growing. We were off between Christmas and New Year's and when we came back I was called into the owner's office and laid off.

I didn't see any signs of a problem. The owners had expected to receive funding from a new "angel," but the funding fell through. The dot-com bubble had burst and money was in short supply. I was offered a decent severance package of one month's income plus vacation time, provided I agreed to sign over my stake in the company. I took the money and ran. Within six months all but the owners had been laid off. The rest were not offered a similar severance package.

When I took the job with the dot-com start-up I knew I was taking a huge risk. I figured either the company would take off and I'd strike it rich (as was the case with many dot-com babies involved with such successful start-ups as Google, Yahoo!, and

Amazon), or I'd be left to fend for myself. Unfortunately for me, the latter was the case.

But since I was aware of the possibility of total failure, I continued to build my online writing business on the side. I had been saving money to put toward starting my own business. The layoff happened with only six months income saved, but my business plans were already in place. The layoff gave me the incentive I needed to take a risk on myself.

Today, that writing business is very successful with more than twenty-five books in the market. Had the dot-com been successful, I don't know if I ever would have taken the risk. But I do know that I love being my own boss and setting my own priorities each day—and I also love never having to worry about being laid off again.

Starting a business may not be your dream, but whatever you wish for yourself, don't think that the company you work for will worry about helping you fulfill your dream. Always keep your eye on what you want and always prepare for what's next. Of course, I'm not saying you shouldn't put your best effort into wherever you're working. Good references are critical for your next job and you'll only get them if you perform well in your current position. Just don't get comfortable where you are. Always keep an eye on your next opportunity so you don't miss it when it comes along and so you're ready if and when your company decides to downsize and show you the door.

- Setting the layoff scene
- Early warning signs
- Your legal rights

CHAPTER 1

"Your Position Has Been Eliminated"

SOMETIMES YOU TURN on the morning news and discover your company will be laying off people. When you arrive at work you feel as though you are walking into a morgue. Other times, you walk through the doors and see everyone whispering in the coffee room, looking anxious or depressed. Rumors are spreading that a major layoff will be announced that day.

These scenarios are common in major layoffs. In a minor layoff, you may not see anything coming until your boss calls you into his office. Decisions were made privately at some higher level about budget cuts and no one saw it coming.

Whether you are part of a mass layoff or one of a just a few, you initially face feelings of depression and anger. You'll essentially move through all the steps of mourning a loss.

In this chapter you'll learn about the state of employment (or unemployment) in the United States. You'll come to identify layoff signs and understand your legal rights. When it comes to that awful layoff moment, you'll find surefire ways to negotiate your severance package and a list of the things you should take with you as you leave—if you're given the opportunity to go back to your office.

Laid Off in America

Layoffs in the United States are becoming more and more common as companies determine that employees are disposable and no longer see the value of experienced workers with a long-term company history. Often a company only realizes the value lost by laying off someone with twenty years of experience when it's too late and that worker is long gone. Occasionally someone with a strong institutional knowledge will be called back as a consultant after a layoff, but don't count on that happening to you. If you were laid off, it's time to move on to greener pastures.

While it may be tempting to go back if you are recalled, remember unless your company undergoes a major shift, it's most likely just a matter of time before it downsizes again, especially in an economic downturn. If you've been laid off, it's probably best to be off that sinking ship and focusing your energy on your next best opportunity.

Each month between July 2004 and June 2008, there were at least 1,100 mass layoff events in the United States according to the seasonally adjusted figures of the U.S. Department of Labor. More than 100,000 people filed for an initial unemployment claim each of those months. The month with the fewest number of layoff events was October 2005 with 1,101 mass layoff events and 110,035 new initial unemployment claimants. September 2005 held the record for the most layoff events: 2,248 with 257,544 new initial unemployment claims. So if you've been laid off, you certainly are not alone.

Spotting a Layoff

So, how do you know if a layoff is imminent? There are many signs you can look for both inside and outside your company. Maybe your workload had been unusually light. That's a classic sign of a layoff in the wings. This happened to a friend of mine. When she returned to work after being on vacation, she learned there had been a layoff. Luckily she escaped that cut, but it indicated that she should start keeping her eye open for other opportunities. The company's sales had decreased and fewer projects were expected, so they were forced to make budget cuts.

While a lighter workload is one of the most obvious signs of a company's need to downsize, here are some other things to watch to help you stay clued-in to a potential layoff:

First, look inside your company. Listen to the company gossip, but don't believe everything you hear. When you hear gossip of a pending layoff, look for signs that justify the rumors, such as budget tightening, travel canceled, hiring freezes, senior management firings, unfamiliar faces (potential buyers) being paraded around the office. A request for proposals from outplacement firms also gives you a clue that change is on the horizon.

Next, follow news about the industry and look for stories that specifically mention your company. You may find analysts reporting about flagging sales, improper behavior by management, a possible SEC investigation, or problems with key products.

Read reports put out by your company. Always read coverage of quarterly and annual reports if you work for a public company. The quarterly reports are "10-Q" and the annual reports are "10-K." All public companies must file these reports with the U.S. Securities and Exchange Commission (SEC). Most companies post these reports on their websites in the Investor Relations section. If your company doesn't, you can use the EDGAR search tool at *www.sec.gov* to find it. Pay attention to news about the company's profit margins and sales. If the news looks bleak, ramp up your job search.

Find out whether insiders are buying or selling your company's stock. A good place to check that is at *www.finance.yahoo.com.* Search for your company. On its summary page you will see a list on the left. In the "Ownership" section look for the link to "Insider Transactions." If you find that many of the major insiders are selling the stock, it would be wise to start looking for a new job.

Check the stock price. If the stock price for your company goes down month after month, it's usually a sign of trouble. The market could be wrong, but it might be right.

Watch for signs that your company is on the chopping block. You may read stories about offers being made to take over your company. After a sale there are often layoffs as the two companies merge or the acquiring company makes its mark. At the very least you can expect that duplicate staffs such as human resources, finance, and sales will be combined. Usually the people in the company that was bought out are the first to be laid off.

Even if you don't start looking, it's time to be sure you make a list of all your contacts that you may want to stay in touch with if you are let go. These can be people you work with at the company or outside vendors, clients, or freelancers.

Always keep a backup copy of your contacts list at home. That's a good practice to start from the day you start a job. You never know when you will arrive at your last day, and may need to reach out to the network you've built.

If you suspect a layoff, start taking home copies of projects you may want to use to show prospective employers, but don't break any confidentiality rules in the process! That could get you fired even if the layoff never materializes.

Also, review your annual employee reviews and make a list of your accomplishments. Quantify your successes. This will be much easier to do when you still have access to your records, so it's a good idea to keep a journal at home where you can record successes (include key details about the project, your role in project, and actual results). You'll be much better prepared for future interviews if this information is noted in a journal. So many people don't record this information and then forget the needed details, or forget about the successful project completely when they're feeling stressed out and looking for a new job. You can use your journal to remind yourself of your successes and help to build the confidence you need as you embark on your job search.

An Unexpected Downsizing

Sometimes you may never see or hear any warnings about a layoff. This is more common in small, privately held companies where the key details about the success or failure of the company are known by only a select few. The company owners look at their year-end results and do some soul-searching to figure out what they think is possible for the next year. Then they make some hard choices.

When I was let go from the dot-com, I was actually lucky to be included in the first wave of layoffs, since others didn't get such generous severance packages as I did. We received a month's severance plus vacation pay in exchange for signing away our right to stock in the company. I took the money and ran. I was already saving money to start my own business and the layoff gave me the kick in the butt I needed to take that risk.

Others who were not laid off and stayed were the unlucky ones. They had to do the work of those of us that had been fired and ultimately got laid off within three months without a severance package. The owners hoped to find additional funding, but it never materialized. The owners kept the company going for many years and built it themselves until they could staff up again, but that was several years later.

Another common scenario where there will be no warning is when a company decides to lay off a small number of people in one particular division.

Even if you've had no warning, if you keep networking contacts at home as well as a journal of your job successes, you should be well-prepared to develop an impressive resume and get started on launching a successful job search.

Know Your Legal Rights

Unfortunately, most people today are "at-will" employees, which pretty much means you can be fired at the whim of your employer. Only the state of Montana looks out for their employees with a "universal for cause protection" clause that comes into effect once workers pass their probationary period. "At-will" employees work at the pleasure of their employer with no definite terms and can be let go for any lawful reason or for no reason at all.

Unless you live in Montana, the only exceptions to "at-will" employment are:

- union workers with a strong collective bargaining agreement;
- public sector workers who are not in management; and
- workers with an employment contract that grants due process.

You also don't have the right to know why you've been terminated unless you live in Maine, Minnesota, or Missouri. Only in those states must an employer provide you with a written statement indicating the reasons for termination. In most states the employer only has to say, "you're fired." You can get a lawyer to try to find out more, but in forty-six states you'll just be wasting your money.

Discrimination

You do have some protections. You can't be fired for reasons of discrimination because of your race, color, sex, age, religion, or disability. If you believe you have been discriminated against and it falls into one of these protected classes you can file a claim with the U.S. Equal Employment Opportunity Commission (*www.eeoc.gov*).

In additional to federal laws, some states have stricter laws that prohibit employment discrimination, so it's worth checking with your state department of labor as well. You do need to act fast if you do want to take legal action; for most discrimination claims, you must file within 180 days from the time you were terminated. In some cases, the deadline can be extended to up to 300 days if the charge involved is also covered by state or local anti-discrimination law.

When filing a discrimination claim with the EEOC you will need:

1. The date or dates the discrimination occurred and a description of each separate discriminatory action. If you believe you are being discriminated against, start keeping a journal with this information as soon as possible.
2. Your name, address, and telephone, as well as the names, addresses, and telephone numbers of the victims of discrimination (if you are not the only one).
3. You will also need the name, address, and telephone number of the organization that you allege committed the acts of discrimination, as well as the total number of employees in that organization.

WARNing

The law that protects employees in a mass firing is called the Worker Adjustment and Retraining Notification (WARN) Act. Any employer who employs more than 100 people and plans a large reduction in force must give its workers a sixty-day notification. WARN became federal law on February 4, 1989.

To fall under the WARN Act, the layoff must result in an employment loss at the single site of employment during any thirty-day period. To qualify under the WARN Act, the layoff can look like any of the following:

A plant closing, which includes shutting down a facility or operating unit within a single site of employment and results in the removal of a minimum of fifty full-time employees.

Mass layoff that includes fifty to 499 employees if they represent at least 33 percent of the total active workforce at a single site of employment, excluding part-time employees.

Mass layoff that includes 500 or more full-time employees. In this case the 33 percent rule does not apply.

If your employer does not "WARN" you, you could be eligible for damages including back pay and benefits for up to sixty days, depending on how much time you were given between the notice of layoff and your last day of pay.

You are entitled to WARN protection if you are terminated, but not if you voluntarily quit, retire, or are discharged for cause. You can also get protection if you are laid off for more than six months or have your work reduced by more than half during any six-month period.

You are not eligible for WARN protection if:

- You are a striker or worker that was locked out in a labor dispute.
- You are working temporarily on a project.
- You are a business partner, consultant, or contract employee.
- You are a federal, state, or local government employee.

When you get that WARNing notice, it should explain whether that layoff or closing is permanent or temporary (six months or less). It should also include the date of layoff or closing and the date of your separation. Sometimes you will get a WARN notice, even if you never get laid off. If the company is downsizing, it may use the WARN notice to encourage attrition or early retirement. If enough people leave voluntarily, you may not get laid off. Your employer can also extend the notice when the date of a planned plant closing or mass layoff changes. If the change of date is fewer than sixty days in the future, then your employee should notify you as soon as possible, reference the first notice, and indicate the new action dates. If the extension is for more than sixty days, your employer must do a new sixty-day warning.

A close friend of mine was part of this type of layoff when he was working full-time for a telecommunications company. The company planned to shut down a division and wanted him to stay past the end date to help with billing after the division closed. The company wasn't sure how long this would take, but to get him to stick around until the bitter end, he was promised a larger package—to the tune of one month severance (rather than the one week offered to those who didn't stay) for every year he worked (plus the cash value of his vacation and sick time). He'd been with the company five years, so that still gave him plenty of money to look for something else after his job ended.

If you're offered a deal like this, it can't hurt to stay around and start networking while you're there. Everyone you work with both inside and outside the company knows what's happening, and if they don't—make sure they do. Keep your eyes and ears open for new opportunities. If a great opportunity comes along take it, but if you can put off your start date to get the extra severance, then why not stay until the end?

If the only notice you receive is a verbal announcement at an employee meeting, that will not satisfy "WARN"ing requirements. Nor will preprinted notices included in your paycheck or pay envelope or press releases announcing the closure in the media.

There are three circumstances that allow a company to avoid the sixty-day notice requirement:

A "faltering company" is not required to give notice of a layoff or plant closing when, before the plant closing, it is actively seeking capital or business, which if obtained would allow the company to avoid or postpone the layoff or closure. Also the company believes that giving the notice in advance could hurt its ability to find the capital or business it needs to continue operating.

A company did not foresee the business circumstances that led to the layoff or closing at the time the sixty-day notice would have been required. For example, a major customer cancels a large order unexpectedly and a plant has to shut down as a result.

A natural disaster leads to an unexpected layoff or plant closing after a hurricane, flood, earthquake, tornado, storm, drought, or other natural disaster.

If you think you have been laid off without proper WARNing, you will need to contact an attorney to assert your rights. If your lawsuit is successful, the employer will generally be required to pay your legal fees, but if you're not successful you will have to pay legal fees out of pocket. To keep your costs down, you may want to contact others who were laid off and are interested in joining you in your case against the company. That way, if you are not successful you have someone with whom to share the fees.

Often an attorney who believes you have a good cause of action will take the case on a contingency, which means he gets a percentage of your award if you win, but gets nothing if the suit is unsuccessful.

The Awful Moment

Whether or not you've received a notice, the actual moment of layoff is traumatic for everyone. If you've hated your job your initial reaction may be that of relief and joy, but quickly reality sets in—you're still out of work and have lost a regular paycheck. Most people feel mixed emotions—anger, depression, relief, joy, anxiety, helplessness, vulnerability, nervousness, revenge, elation, fear, and more fear.

If you're given the chance you may share a few tears and hugs with coworkers, but often a company will escort you out the door immediately after you're given notice. Or, even worse, you could be escorted to your office with a guard who watches your every move as you pack your personal belongings. This can be particularly demeaning, as it seems as if your employer does not trust you. But in reality companies got into the habit of doing this because so many people wiped out computer files or committed acts of sabotage that made it difficult for others to continue working on the laid off employee's projects.

If you're leaving as part of a mass layoff or plant closing, you probably can't wait to get out the door on your last day. You've had sixty days to think about it and just stuck around for the money and severance package. Hopefully you've used that time wisely by networking. Hopefully you've also gradually taken home the information about contacts and projects that you can use to make your job search easier.

MY STORY

I experienced my worst layoff moment when I was working for a small, private nonprofit center affiliated with a university. The morning of my layoff, as I dropped off a report in my boss's empty office, I saw my termination letter on her computer screen.

I was shocked, but immediately started to make calls. I quietly collected relevant contacts and project details. I also gathered samples of projects that I wanted to showcase as I sought a new job. I copied everything to a disk as opposed to e-mailing them so that I'd have no problems taking it all home.

In between crying jags, I called my friends to let them know. I actually ended up talking to several of them during the day to help me keep my cool and get ideas for the best way to handle the exit interview.

I had all day to prepare, as I wasn't laid off until the end of the day that Friday (a traditional layoff time because the remaining staff doesn't find out until the next Monday and there isn't time for discussion).

In some ways, the early notice was great, but it was also difficult waiting for the axe to fall. My anger built and I spent a lot of time trying to determine what went wrong. My reviews had been excellent and I had received a raise two months earlier. But despite the swirl of emotions, I knew I needed to remain calm. Making a scene is never a good idea, especially if you are still counting on good references from people at the company.

Finally, at about 4 P.M., I was called into a meeting with my boss and the human resources representative. The meeting was brief. They reviewed two pages of legalese and to this day I'm not exactly sure what was said. I just wanted it to be over. I was led to my office by the guard and given a few minutes to pack my personal belongings. My ID badge and keys were col-

lected and I was escorted out of the building. I was not permit-
ted to contact anyone. This is one of the most degrading ways
to be laid off and I hope you never have to go through it.

When I calmed down a couple of days later I read my termination letter, which was filled with university legalese. But I
suspect my boss wanted to hire a friend, and in order to make
room for this person she had to say that there wasn't enough
work to justify my continued employment. My reviews were
excellent so she couldn't use my work history as an excuse.

As I talked with people from the organization after the layoff,
I discovered that since they discontinued my position in order
to lay me off it took my boss two years to recoup the budget
to replace me. As a result, she worked outrageous hours to get
her work done—as well as mine. In some small way, that satis-
fied my need for revenge.

Most of us tend to want to seek revenge against the person
who wronged us by laying us off. But the person who executes
the layoff is not always the one that made the decision. There
are actually two types of layoffs—personal layoffs (as in my
story) and institutional layoffs.

If you are the victim of an institutional layoff, your boss may
be no more than a lackey doing what he or she was told to do.
In large institutions, the executive committee can decide they
need to lay off a certain number of people and tell each manager
how many people they must let go. If the institution lets people
go based on seniority and you were the last person hired, you'll
be the first one fired no matter how good you are.

Sometimes layoffs are not based on last hired, first fired.
One of my friends thought she was going to be part of a layoff
because she was hired in the last year. But when the layoffs were
finally announced she was not on the list. The company decided
instead to carefully pick the people who they determined were
"troublemakers." The designated troublemakers were people,
whom for one reason or another were not well-liked in the

office. So if you like to stand up for your opinions, you could be putting yourself on the chopping block during a future layoff.

In this situation it was an institutional layoff. Budgets were cut across the board in the company, but the managers of each work site were given a lot of leeway about the employees they let go. Instead of laying people off based on when they were hired, the managers decided to keep the people who fit in the best in the hopes of minimizing morale problems after the downsizing.

Negotiating Your Severance Package

You won't have any control over whether or not you're laid off, but you might be able to negotiate the provisions of your severance package. You definitely have a better chance to negotiate your package if you've been working on a project and your company wants you to promise not to compete in the near term. There will be more about non-compete agreements soon, but first let's look at the things you can ask for as part of a severance package.

Severance Pay

Most employees are "at-will" employees and severance is not required. There is no federal law governing severance pay, so your employer is not obligated to pay it at all. Your employer is only obligated to give you severance pay if it failed to "WARN" you sixty days prior to a plant closing or mass layoff. Also, if you are under a union contract or other type of contract, severance can also be mandatory. That said, most employers do offer some sort of severance ranging from two weeks to six months or more of your current salary plus unused vacation time, sick time, and floating holidays. This can be paid out in one lump sum or based on your regularly scheduled paychecks. In some cases, the separation agreement will indicate that severance will be paid up to six months or until you find other employment, whichever comes first.

If you get the payment in a lump sum, that wad of cash can be both positive and negative. You will likely be eligible to start collecting unemployment immediately if you get a lump sum, but you will lose a significant amount of that cash to income taxes because the IRS taxes that as a bonus. If you're laid off at the beginning of the year and don't earn as much through the year, you'll likely get a good portion of those taxes back. But, if you are laid off at the end of the year and the lump sum increases your salary so that you jump into the next tax bracket, you won't get as much of those taxes back.

If your severance is paid based on your regular paycheck schedule, you won't feel as much of a tax hit, but you likely won't be able to start collecting unemployment until your severance pay runs out. If you have time, your best bet is to talk with your tax advisor prior to a layoff and figure out together which option is better. Your employer may not give you an option, but you want to be ready to make the best decision just in case he does.

Whichever way you are paid, you can stretch those dollars further by asking your employer not to take out voluntary contributions to your 401(k). I don't recommend that you touch your 401(k) money already in the account. That should be rolled over into an individual IRA, which we'll discuss in greater detail in Chapter 3.

Severance or Separation Agreement

At your exit interview, you will likely be handed a severance or separation agreement. At the very least this should specify the amount of your severance pay, the time period over which these payments will be made, and when the payments will end.

You should also find details of what benefits will continue through the severance payment period and when your benefits will end. Health insurance is the most crucial. If your company offers group health insurance, it must continue to provide those benefits for eighteen months after your group benefits end, but you'll be paying for them out of pocket. This requirement is based on a federal law called COBRA.

WHAT IS COBRA?

The Consolidated Omnibus Budget Reconciliation Act (COBRA) gives you and your family protection against losing your health benefits. If you are laid off you have the right to choose to continue group health benefits provided by the company for eighteen months (and in some cases up to thirty-six months) after a job loss, reduction in the hours worked, transition between jobs, death, divorce, and other life events. If you are qualified for COBRA, you may be required to pay the entire premium for coverage up to 102 percent of the cost to the plan.

Generally, if your company has twenty or more employees, COBRA requires that group health plans offer employees and their families the opportunity for a temporary extension of health coverage (called continuation coverage), after employee coverage ends. For example, if you get three months severance that includes continuing health benefits, your COBRA coverage would start after the three-month severance period ends. Your employer must send you a notice explaining the COBRA benefits, the costs of those benefits, and how you must pay for them.

In some cases the health insurance company may be willing to extend benefits beyond COBRA through an individual insurance plan. It's worth asking the question when your COBRA benefits end if you haven't found a job or if the job you did find does not include health benefits.

In addition to information about your final check, your severance pay, your accrued vacation, personal and sick pay, you should also get in writing any entitlement to future commissions and bonuses. For example, if you are a salesperson and completed sales for which you have not yet received commissions or bonuses you want to be sure that the money owed is detailed in writing. Also, if you are due any expenses or reimbursements, those should be indicated in writing as well to protect yourself.

As part of a severance package, some employees offer outplacement services to help you find a job. These services can be offered at many different levels—from helping you write a resume and career counseling to providing you office space for a number of months until you find a job. If your company does offer outplacement services and you don't need them, you may want to call the company that offers the services and find out what they cost. In lieu of accepting those services you may be able to negotiate for a higher lump sum.

Unlike health insurance, if you have employer-provided life insurance, that will usually end on the day you are laid off and there are no obligations for the employer to continue coverage. However, some employers have a continuation option that allows you to maintain life insurance provided you pay for the full costs. Continuation insurance won't be cheap, but if you believe you have a health condition that might make it difficult to get approved for individual life insurance, you may want to consider taking the continuation insurance. The same is true for disability insurance.

Options regarding your retirement plan will vary depending upon the type of plans that are in place with your current employer. Some employers still offer defined benefit plans, which are plans that guarantee a retirement payout for the rest of your life provided you worked the required number of years to be vested in the program (when you own the employer's contribution 100 percent). If your employer does offer a defined benefit plan, be sure you understand the vesting rules and what your ultimate payout will be.

Most companies that do provide a retirement plan today offer defined contribution plans such as a 401(k) or 403(b). For these plans you, and sometimes your employer, makes a contribution toward your retirement savings. There is no guaranteed benefit, but there are rules that govern when your employer's contribution to the 401(k) is fully vested and you get to take it with you. The same is true with profit sharing plans and other employer-sponsored retirement savings plans.

You may want to contact a financial advisor who can review the options you are being given for your retirement plans, as well as the rule governing those plans to be sure you are being offered a fair amount for withdrawing the funds from those plans and rolling them over into an individual retirement savings account such as an IRA. (We'll review these issues in Chapter 3.)

Another key provision that should be covered in your separation agreement is stock options, if you have any. You should receive information explaining your choices about your stocks and your ability to purchase them and for how long you have that ability.

If you have a company car or company laptop, you may be able to work out a favorable deal on these items as well. It never hurts to ask.

In exchange for all these goodies your employer will likely include terms of your layoff that essentially forbids you to disclose trade secrets or hold the company liable for terminating you. The agreement will likely reiterate provisions of any confidentiality agreement you signed when you took the job. You can think of severance agreements as a bribe for keeping you quiet and in some cases even getting you to agree not to compete with the company. When you sign the agreement you are signing a binding contract, so if you are unclear about what you are agreeing to or want to modify that agreement, you may want to contact an attorney before signing anything. You also may want to negotiate some nonmonetary agreements in your favor as well. Here are some key provisions you may find in a severance agreement that don't involve money:

Non-compete clause: If you work in a highly competitive industry, you will likely find a non-compete clause is part of the agreement. You essentially have to agree not to compete with your former company for a certain period of time. Most states regulate the validity of these clauses. In order for them to hold up in court they must be reasonable in their terms and limitations of time and geography. They can't make it impossible for you to work again where you are currently living. If you believe the clause is unreasonable, attempt to negotiate a better deal, but if you are sure you won't be able to find work because of a non-complete clause, contact an attorney before signing it.

Non-disparagement clause: This clause protects both you and your employer. You both agree not to make any derogatory statements about the other to a third party.

Resign in lieu of termination clause: If you are being laid off or fired and prefer that it does not appear on your work record, you could negotiate to resign in lieu of being fired. Be sure that your work record not only shows that you resigned, but also shows that you are eligible for rehire. Sometimes employees use the code that you are not eligible for rehire as a way of raising a red flag for future employers who call for a reference. If your employer is uneasy with coding you for rehire, you can agree in writing that you will not apply for re-employment.

Favorable letter of recommendation: You definitely want to get in writing that your employer will provide a favorable letter of recommendation. Even better, you should draft that letter and get your employer to agree to it prior to signing your separation agreement. As part of this clause you should get an agreement from your employer that they will not deviate from this letter. Some employers give only neutral references. If that is the case make sure your employer puts it in writing. If you find out afterwards that you got a negative reference, you'll have something in writing indicating that your employer violated his own policy.

Unemployment benefits assurance: If you think your employer may contest your unemployment benefits, indicating you were let go for just cause, you may want to ask them to include a clause indicating that your employer will not contest your unemployment benefits.

Liability protection from lawsuits: If you had the type of position where you could be drawn into a lawsuit because of the work you did for the company, you may want to negotiate a clause indicating the company will protect you against any liability related to work you did for the company. For example, if you were a comptroller or chief financial officer and had responsibility for reporting to regulatory agencies, any question about your work could come up after you leave. You want to be sure your company will pay for any legal services you might need to defend yourself against a work-related claim.

Your employer will likely try to avoid putting things in writing. Don't accept verbal promises. They will not stand up in a court of law if you find that you understand the verbal promises differently than your employer understands them. To be safe, always get promises in writing.

On the day you are laid off, especially if you had no inkling it was going to happen, you may not want to sign your severance agreement. Tell your boss you want to seek legal advice before signing. Even if all you do is take it home and let someone who is not as emotional review the document, taking the time to sleep on such a critical document is a wise move. In addition, if there are significant monetary or nonmonetary issues, don't hesitate to consult with an attorney for an hour to have him review the document and be sure you are well protected. If you want changes, you must negotiate those changes before you sign. Once you've signed and agree to the contract, you'll find it nearly impossible to get a change.

Take Your Contact Lists

It bears repeating: The most valuable things you can take with you when you leave your job are your contacts. These are the people who will start the network you will need to find your next job. If you don't already have a copy of your contacts names, addresses, phone numbers, and e-mail addresses at home, print them out or copy them to a flash drive and take them home—as long as you have the time to do so. Since a layoff can happen quickly and you can be out the door before you get a chance to do this, I recommend that you make it a habit to keep a current list of work contacts on your home computer or in a written form. After you leave a friend who is still there may be willing to help you, but don't count on it.

Leaving Your Workplace for the Final Time

Whether you loved the job or hated it, you will feel emotionally drained as you walk out the door of the company for the last time, jobless. Everyone does. Your life has been turned upside down and unless you've already found your next opportunity, you have no idea what you're going to do, how you're going to tell family and friends, and how you'll pick up the pieces. In the next chapter we'll explore how to handle your first week of unemployment.

RECAP: While everyone needs to take whatever amount of time necessary to complete the tasks laid out in the book, I've set it up as a week-by-week process. Don't be discouraged if you need to take longer than a week for the tasks in any chapter. Before you move on to Chapter 2, be sure you:

- Know how to recognize the signs of a layoff, so you can be prepared. If you haven't been laid off, but suspect it could be coming, these signs will help you figure it out.
- Understand your legal rights as an employee, as well as the protections given to you by the WARNing system.
- Review the basics of discrimination claims and whether or not you should file one.
- Explore the options you can seek in regards to severance pay and a severance agreement.
- Get to know your COBRA rights.
- Keep a professional contacts list at home or create one as soon as you can.

- Riding the emotional roller coaster
- Working through the grieving process
- Telling your family and friends

CHAPTER 2

Week 1: Give Yourself Some Time

WHEN YOU WAKE up the first day after being fired, panic sets in. You have nowhere to go and it hits home that you no longer have a paycheck. Most people walk around in a state of shock on the day of the lay off or firing, even if they were expecting the layoff. They feel numb, just making it through the day. Often they wake up the next morning not even knowing how they got home—especially if they went out for drinks with friends the night before.

Day 1 after losing your job is the day you truly start working through the grieving process. Take the time to grieve, just as you would after the loss of a family member or friend. Losing a job can be just as devastating, if not more personally devastating, as losing a loved one. Many of us think of ourselves in terms of our jobs and all of a sudden we feel as if we have lost our identity. In this chapter we'll explore the grieving process most of us experience after a job loss. Then you'll learn how to avoid your natural response to deny your loss and isolate yourself after the loss and instead talk with family and friends. You'll definitely be angry and probably want to bad-mouth your boss and your former company, but I'll uncover why you must avoid that tendency except with only your closest family and friends. Once we get through all of the emotional stuff, we'll focus on what you should do to survive your first week of your new life.

The Grieving Process

How you will work through the loss of a job is not that much different from any other type of mourning. You'll pass through these five stages:

1. Denial and isolation
2. Anger
3. Bargaining
4. Depression
5. Acceptance

This may not be a linear progression. Some people move right to anger and then when they calm down move toward denial and isolate themselves. Many people will move through a stage and then go back to it a few days later because of a particular setback or conversation with a friend or family member. Don't think you're not making progress if you get past the anger, make yourself a bargain with God about how you'll start going to services every week if he helps you get a job, and then fall back into anger when the job doesn't just appear. It's normal to move back and forth through these stages of mourning until you finally get to acceptance. Even at acceptance you may slip backward if you get excited about a job interview, expecting to get the position and it falls through.

Let's take a closer look at what you might expect to find in each of the stages of mourning.

Denial and Isolation

Often the first emotion you feel is to deny the layoff ever happened. This is normal. You try to rationalize that it didn't happen because it just can't happen to you. You start thinking that after about a week they'll realize that they can't possibly get all your work done and they'll call you back in desperation.

Unfortunately, none of us are indispensable and even if things are difficult at the workplace after a layoff, the company expects that to happen. The people who were not let go will all be overworked and stressed out as they try to get their own work done, as well as the work passed on to them as the managers divvy up the work of those laid off. Some may even quit in protest because they just can't handle the stress or they expect they could be next. It's common for morale to slip after a layoff, so even as you are moving through the stages of mourning, I can guarantee those still at work aren't feeling great, either.

But don't give in to this denial. You have lost your job. You won't likely be called back (unless you're in an industry where temporary layoffs are common when the work is slow). You need to accept it and move on.

As part of this denial, you think you should isolate yourself and not tell anyone. You may think that if you don't talk about it the problem will go away. Wouldn't it be great if that were true? But it's not. Isolating yourself will not help and can only pave your path to depression.

Avoid the tendency to isolate yourself. Try to keep to your daily exercise routine or even increase the time you spend on exercise. Exercise has been shown to improve self-esteem. When you exercise, your body actually releases a chemical called endorphins. These endorphins help reduce the pain you're feeling from your job loss. Endorphins trigger a positive feeling in the body, which can have a similar effect to that of morphine. After a run or workout, many people will feel almost euphoric.

That feeling is known as a "runner's high" and it can give you a more positive outlook on life.

WHAT ARE ENDORPHINS?

Scientifically researchers have found that endorphins act as analgesics, which mean that they diminish the perception of pain. They can also act as sedatives, so if you haven't been getting a lot of sleep after your job loss, exercise may be able to help you solve that problem too.

Endorphins are manufactured in your brain, spinal cord and many other parts of the body and are released in response to brain chemicals called neurotransmitters. The neuron receptors endorphins bind themselves to are the same ones that bind some pain medicines. However, unlike morphine, when the body activates these endorphins it does not lead to the same risks of addiction or dependence.

Now don't expect this to be a miracle cure, but over time you will feel the benefits of this exercise. Make sure you pursue an exercise you enjoy and you'll come home feeling better than when you left the house. Regular exercise can help you:

- Reduce stress
- Minimize feelings of depression
- Reduce anxiety
- Boost self-esteem
- Improve sleep

These are all the things you need to help you bounce back after a layoff. You'll also enjoy some other key health benefits that can't hurt. Exercise will:

- Strengthen your heart
- Increase energy levels

- Lower blood pressure
- Improve muscle tone and strength
- Reduce body fat
- Make you look more fit and healthy, which of course can only help you get that next job

So instead of hiding or isolating yourself, get out and exercise. You may even find some new exercise buddies that can join your network and help you find your next job.

This first stage of denial and isolation is a normal reaction to rationalize what's just happened to you. It is a defense mechanism that helps to buffer you from the shock you've just experienced. This defense mechanisms helps you block out reality and hide from the fact that you've just lost your job. You'll find it helps you live through the initial pain from your job loss.

Anger

As the masking feelings of denial and isolation begin to fade, you'll likely move toward the stage of anger. That's when the reality of the loss of your job and the pain you initially felt resurfaces. You're not quite ready to accept the loss, so this intense emotion comes from our most vulnerable core and we strike back in anger.

You might find yourself striking inanimate objects (much safer than people around you as long as you don't hurt yourself) or striking out at family and friends (be careful, someone could get hurt whether you strike out physically or verbally). You probably feel guilty for being angry toward family and friends and this makes you even angrier.

Don't be frightened by the anger you'll feel about your job loss. That's normal and you do need to exhaust that anger before you can start looking for another job. If you don't take control of that anger, it will take control of you and ruin any chances you have of finding that next job and it could possibly even ruin your relationships with your family and friends. You'll put off negative vibes and turn off everyone around you.

You'll certainly be asking yourself a lot of these questions as you find ways to channel your anger:

- Why was my boss out to get me?
- Was he threatened by my work?
- Did he use me as a scapegoat?
- Did he blame me for something that he did wrong?
- How did I miss signs that this was coming?
- If not, why did I ignore them?

I've probably just barely scratched the surface of questions you'll be asking as you sort through your anger. Don't stop. Get it all out. Write it all down. You may even find it helpful to write your ex-boss a long letter spewing all this anger out on paper—but don't mail it!

After writing that letter, read it the next morning. Does it sound logical to you? What would happen if that letter ended up in the hands of someone who was thinking of hiring you? Would they hire you? Most likely not. No one wants to hire an angry, bitter person. That's why it's important for you to take the time and write down your anger and work through it before you start looking for another job.

Give yourself a day or two to sort through that anger if needed. When you've gotten through that rage, you then need to document what happened. Try to remove all the emotion that you're feeling from losing your job and just write down the account of what happened. This will be easier to do if the layoff was an institutional layoff where many people were let go. If you were one of only a few it will be a lot harder to separate the emotions from the facts.

Let's start with the facts. How many were let go? Were they all from the same department? Were they all of a certain age?

Were they all new hires? Is the economy down? Was the workload getting lighter and lighter? Did the company lose a major customer? Carefully work through the reasons for the layoff as you try to understand them.

After you write down all the basic facts, you'll then need to dig a lot deeper to figure out why you were the one chosen. Quickly look back to when you took the job. Were you excited about the opportunity for growth or did you take the job just to make the money you needed? If you were passionate about the job, did you lose that passion as you found out what it was like to work that job, day in and day out? Did the job requirements change and your skills were no longer as valuable? If you lost enthusiasm for the job it may have contributed to your being selected as one of the employees to be laid off.

Did you work well with your co-workers or were you someone who constantly created tension in the workplace? People who don't fit in often will be the first laid off. You need to do some soul searching and make sure you didn't contribute to your selection by your actions.

Think about the things you could have done to perform better at your workplace. In reality, the reasons for being laid off usually involve things that happened in the industry that created a need for a reduction in workforce, things that involve your boss and his or relationship with his boss, and things that involve your relationship between you and your boss, as well as the type of job you did. Rarely do only one of these factors come into play unless you were laid off because a plant closed. Even when a department or division is shut down, those workers who are most valued are usually offered something else in the company. So you do need to face reality even after a layoff that your actions probably contributed to the layoff decision. You do need to look at yourself and your actions, so you can be sure not to repeat those actions in your next job.

Now take these facts you've pulled together and develop a story about the layoff that you can tell family and friends. You may want to work up a second, much shorter story that you can use when you start networking for a new job or start interviewing. Practice telling your story to the mirror and watch your facial expressions. At first you may show anger or tears, but as you get more used to telling the story it will become easier and easier. While family and friends may accept your anger immediately after a layoff, if you continue to be bitter about it, you will begin to turn them off.

Bargaining

Bargaining is the phase in which you start taking back control. This can be the fun stage. You start making all kinds of bargains with yourself and maybe even with God to help you get a job faster. Even people who are not religious may find themselves playing the God card. While faith is very important, you have to remember that God helps those who help themselves.

In reality, what you are doing is a normal phase of grieving for a loss. You feel helpless and vulnerable and need to regain control of the situation. You start thinking things like, "If I'd only done such and such maybe such and such won't have happened." You fill in those "such and such" items based on whatever fits.

You can take this stage as a respite before going on to the hard work ahead. This stage helps you weather the difficult stage ahead. But sometimes it can also lead us to depression.

Depression

As we realize our bargains are just not working and we truly face the job loss, it is common to next move into depression. As discussed above, exercise can be one of the best medicines to help you push through this phase. And, you will feel like you are pushing a huge stone up a large hill and moving almost nowhere.

You may start sleeping ten to twelve hours a day or maybe not sleeping at all. You'll find that sadness and regret will dominate your thought processes. You'll start worrying about how you can pay the bills and put food on your table—and everything else you normally pay for with the salary you no longer can depend upon.

Your family and friends will wonder how they can help you work through this phase. Many times just a few hugs and words of kindness and support can be the best medicine. If you do find yourself unable to get out of bed after about a week or so, don't hesitate to contact your doctor. Don't feel as though it's a weakness if you are not able to rise above the depression alone. Sometimes medication can lift a deep depression and help you get back to doing what you need to do—start looking for a new job.

If you allow depression to take hold, you won't have the energy or the confidence you need to look for a job. You won't make a good impression during an interview and you won't get a job. Doing whatever you need to do to lift those feelings of depression can be the most important thing you'll need to do before you can start an active job search.

Acceptance

When you finally accept your job loss, you'll find the depression tends to lift and you now have the energy to look for that next opportunity. Don't be disheartened if you slip back into depression after looking for work for a while. You may find that each time you get a rejection letter you begin to head down a slippery slope and may even fall all the way back to denial and isolation, especially when you put your heart and soul into a particular job or the rejection was from your first choice company.

Don't get discouraged. You'll find yourself moving through the steps of grief much quicker as you take the baby steps you need to take to get that next job. (We'll delve into the job search process in Chapters 4 through 9.)

What you need to work on during the first week of unemployment is yourself. Get yourself into a state of mind that will allow you to start thinking of the future rather than rehashing what happened the day you lost your job or why you lost your job. You do need to face that head on, but it cannot become your main focus. Some key things you must remember to move past the stages of grief include:

- *Stay active*—don't give up all your activities and mourn.
- *Establish a new routine*—you were forced to change your daily routine because of the job loss. Establish a new daily routine as quickly as you can so you don't focus solely on the job loss, but start looking toward the future.
- *Nurture yourself*—you need to get an adequate amount of sleep (but don't spend your entire day in bed). Eat healthy meals, exercise, and always make time for something fun every day as you look for a new job.
- *Avoid taking on additional stress*—sometimes people will want to help you stay busy so they suggest you take on a major project for your community or your church or synagogue. While you may want to get involved in something, this is not the time to take on a leadership role. You need to focus on yourself and what you want to do next. Leading a major project and the focus you need to get you started may feel good, but it won't put food on your table and it won't likely help you find that next job.
- *Respect the time you need for grieving*—there is no right way to grieve or timetable for that grief. It's different for everyone.

- *Don't be afraid to ask for help*—seek psychological or spiritual counseling if needed to help you get through the grieving process.

Telling Your Spouse

Your first task after being laid off will be to tell your family. Some people dread this so much that they continue to prepare for work and leave the house each day as if going to work. They will keep this charade up for as long as they can. Don't fall into that temptation. It may be hard for you to tell your spouse and face his or her anger, disappointment, anxiety, fear—the whole host of emotions you will likely face. You certainly don't need that because you're feeling the same things yourself, but sharing the news and comforting each other is the best thing you can do for yourself.

If you're married, wait until you get home to break the news. You may be tempted to call from work, but this is not the kind of news best relayed over the phone. If your spouse breaks down and needs a hug, you won't be there for him or her. You know how shocking this news was for you. It will be equally shocking for your spouse.

Telling your spouse by telephone if he or she is currently in a public place can be truly devastating for a number of reasons. He or she could break down and make a bad impression there, creating an embarrassing scene. You both will likely drive home upset, risking an accident. You may find it hard to wait, but it's better for you to talk in the privacy of your home.

Remember, this will hit your spouse almost as personally as you. By the time you tell your spouse, you will have had time to sort through some of your initial emotions, but give him or her time to digest the news and feel what will likely be similar emotions. You may expect to find comfort and support, but instead the initial response may be anger. As you assist your spouse in comprehending the initial shock that you lost your job, you will be helping yourself work through the emotions as well.

Don't try to solve the problem with this initial conversation. You need to communicate the situation clearly, but you're certainly not ready for answers to any of the questions that your spouse will likely ask, such as, "How will we pay the bills?" or "What will we do now?" Answer truthfully that you don't know, but that you want to work on this together. Assure your spouse that the family will be okay and that your first priority will be to find a solution.

Depending upon your spouse's personality:

- The reaction could be one of comfort and support, or
- He or she may be someone who wants to work on fixing the problem immediately.

If your spouse starts coming up with lots of ideas and you're not ready to deal with them, let him or her know you need some time to absorb the shock and process the pain and anger before you start working on solutions. It's important to allow the emotions of the loss flow during the first week after a layoff. If you jump too quickly to take the first job you can find without thinking through your options, you likely will take a job that you're not happy with and be back in the same boat just a few months down the road.

If there was tension in the marriage or relationship before your layoff, the impact of the job loss could exacerbate the situation. Remember, a job loss is stressful not only for you, but for all who were depending on your paycheck. You may find that your partner lashes out at you for not doing enough in finding another job before the layoff—especially if you discussed signs of a problem at work with him or her and didn't act quickly to find something else.

Telling Your Kids

Even harder than telling your partner or spouse will be telling your children, if you have them. How to break the news to them depends on their age and what they are capable of understanding. The key thing they want to know is that everything will be all right. You need to let them know you'll be around the house more, which may or may not be good news. Younger children may be very excited to be able to spend more time with you. If you have teenagers, they may hate the fact and fear that they'll lose some of their freedoms. You will have to tell them that the family needs to cut back on expenses, so you won't be going out to eat as much or buying them as many toys or new clothes. You may also have to reduce or halt their allowance for a while.

Whatever decisions you make as you work through this loss, keep your kids in the loop at whatever level they can understand. How much they will understand will depend on their age.

Four- to Six-Year-Olds

Your kids will have some understanding that you go out to work, but will not understand how devastating the loss of a job is to you. If you say you are fired, they might take it literally and think you were set ablaze. If you say you are laid off, they could picture you're being pushed off a bed or some other literal image.

As with the younger aged children, they won't fully understand but they will feel the tension and they will see the changes. They know you were leaving the house every day and now you are home. You may find that their anxieties manifest themselves in actions like loss of bladder control, loss of appetite, or sleeping disorders.

Encourage them to talk about and listen to the fears they are experiencing. Their fears could be totally untrue and you may be able to alleviate them just by comforting them and explaining things to them.

Seven-to Twelve-Year Olds

Your kids will definitely understand the meaning of a job loss and may even have been part of a take your child to work day, but they won't really understand how devastating this can be for you. Respond to their questions truthfully and be sure to check in with them regularly to see how they are doing.

They will enjoy having you around, but may not understand that you need quiet time to work on finding a new job. As they see the tension build in the house they could become very clingy, so be careful about how you keep them away when you need to work quietly on your job search.

You may see signs of problems in school, learning problems, antisocial behavior, hypochondria, or unusual aggression as they work through the tensions they see in the home. Don't get angry. Instead, take the time to talk with them and assure them that all will be okay. They know there is a change, but don't fully understand its impact.

Teens

Your teenagers will be very aware of what a job loss means. They may even have worked and earned money. But they tend to be self-absorbed and will be worried about how it's going to affect them and the money they count on. You may see some of the same behavioral problems that you see in seven- to twelve-year-olds, but you'll find it much harder to get them to talk about what's bothering them. Be patient. Their hormones are raging and their emotions are all over the map. Their primary concerns will be concerns about moving, changing schools, leaving their friends, inability to buy things they want, or having to delay going on to college. Just let them know that you will try to keep changes to the very minimum and will include them in discussions if major changes are needed.

Older teens think they are already adults and don't like being left out of the decision-making process. So even if you don't intend to include them as you try to make career choices that might include a move, do give them a chance to talk about it before you let them know the decision is made so they feel as though they've had a say in their lives.

Grown Children

Your kids who have left the nest are going to worry about you. They know what you are going through and may have experienced something similar to what you are now going through. Their concerns will be about how you are doing and whether you may need help financially, if they are in a position to help out. They'll be concerned about how you are coping and may become a part of your emotional support network.

Don't put up a wall and block them out. While they may be adults and out on their own, you're still their parent and they still need to be part of your life. They may never have seen you go through a layoff and may get very worried about your coping skills. Let them in and let them help in whatever way they can. It will only strengthen your bond with them.

Teach Your Kids How to Deal with Adversity

The actions you take and how open you are with your children can be a very valuable lesson, or it can foster fear. Keep them involved as you work on your job search and show them how to handle times of anxiety and fear.

Even if you don't try to teach them, they will be learning lessons about how to deal with adversity by how you do it. If they see you acting defeated, angry and overwhelmed by stress, that's likely how they will deal with adversity in the future. If they see you work calmly through the process of finding a new job, that's the lesson they will learn.

Thinking of this process as a course in how to deal with adversity for your children may help you regain control of the situation. As you try to put on a positive face for your kids, you'll gradually get into the habit of truly feeling more positive.

Let your kids know that setbacks and disappointments are just a part of life, but one needs to move on to bigger and better challenges. Trying to hide the problem and how you deal with it from your kids won't teach them anything. Instead, they'll probably notice the tension you're feeling and think they did something wrong.

Telling Your Friends

Telling your family is tough because layoffs can incur significant changes to their everyday lives. Telling your friends can be tough for different reasons because your self-esteem and confidence is on the line, but don't get caught up in denial or subterfuge. Remember, you'll need your friends to help find your next job. Friends also serve as a valuable support network.

You'll need to make a list of which friends you want for emotional support and which friends you want to call on for your job search. The ones you want for emotional support are the ones you should tell first as you work through your emotions immediately after a job loss. To these people, you should feel comfortable expressing the anger and disappointment you feel. Talk about your lack of confidence, which may be festering under your skin and you can't show to your family.

This emotional support network may be just what you need as you move into the stages of denial, anger, and depression. But don't lean on them too much because friends may start pulling away if they don't see you making progress. A truly good friend will know when you need professional help to move to the next stage (especially if you're caught in denial or depression). Others might just find ways to avoid you because they are tired of hearing your tirades about the company or the job loss or can't tolerate being around someone so depressed or unwilling to accept reality.

Two-Way Street

Don't become so self-absorbed that you miss signs that someone in your emotional support network needs support. Keep yourself open to their needs as well. Sometimes helping a friend can do more to lift your spirits and regain your self-confidence than talking about your own problems. You need to keep a careful balance of dealing with your issues, as well as helping your friends with theirs.

You may find you need to encourage your friends to share their good news with you, such as information about a promotion or a new job. They may be afraid it will not be helpful since you're going through such a rough time. Let your friends know you want to hear their good news because it helps to lift your mood. Positive energy helps even if it involves someone else's good fortune. When someone tells you good news, be sure to share in their excitement or you will be thought of as a buzz kill and people will avoid you when they have good news.

Once you're feeling ready to start looking for work—and do wait until you've got your anger under control and are starting to regain some confidence—you'll be ready to contact those friends and acquaintances that you think will become part of your job search network. As I discussed above, have your story ready about why you lost your job and be ready to discuss it without showing anger or breaking down in tears. You want to approach this network of people in strength so they will feel comfortable giving you additional contacts and help you build your job search network. We'll talk more about networking in Chapter 5.

Things You Shouldn't Do

Resist the temptation to act out in ways that might feel right at the time, but when you look back, will seem impulsive at best and destructive at worse. It's important to take this week to sit with your feelings and digest what's happened, otherwise you'll find it difficult to form a plan of action that will carry you through later weeks. Here are a few scenarios to avoid at all costs.

Don't Bad-Mouth the Company

Don't blow up at your former company and start bad-mouthing them all over the place, especially by posting on job boards on the Internet or any other public place. This will come back to haunt you as you start looking for a job. Many employers today will do a search of online postings to find out what you think personally. Remember: Anything you post online on public job boards may be seen by a potential future employer.

Outside your closest network of family and friends do not under any circumstances bad-mouth the company and your former boss. The friends on your list for emotional support are the only ones with whom you should feel comfortable expressing your anger. This is because you'll find that most industries are very incestuous. Anything you say could get back to your company and burn your bridges in such a way that you won't be able to count on them for a decent reference. You also could end up running into a close friend of your ex-boss as you build your job search network. If you say something bad about your former boss, you could turn off someone who may have been a great source of job leads. In addition, when you're on an interview, if you bad-mouth your former company, the person sitting on the other side of the desk could see you as a troublemaker and question whether it's a good idea to take a risk with you.

Even though you're angry and may like the idea of destroying your former employer, don't give in to that feeling. Angry people don't get hired. Be sure you work through your anger before you embark on a job search.

Don't Jump Into a New Job Search

The worst thing that you can do during your first week of unemployment is panic and start looking for work. I can guarantee if you do get hired, it won't be what you want to do long-term unless it's a job you've been trying to get for many months and you just happen to get a request for an interview. Even if that's the case, you won't be able to put your best foot forward while you are still trying to deal with the emotions of getting laid off.

Even if you are going to interview with someone who knows you've been laid off, try to schedule the interview for the next week to give yourself some time to reduce the stress and anger you're feeling. You'll then be more prepared to make a great impression.

Don't Burn Through Your Severance

Definitely don't plan that expensive cruise or other vacation you've been wanting because you now have that nice lump sum severance check in your pocket. While that might give you great initial satisfaction, it will set you up for financial disaster when you come home. Do take a brief, inexpensive vacation if you need to reduce stress, but keep the expenses as low as possible. You'll need the money when you get back until you find something else.

Don't Give in to Depression

Don't get into bed for a few days and decide you never want to get out. You will find that depression is like getting caught in a whirlpool, as you get drawn further and further down into the depths of darkness. Push yourself to get out of bed and do something you enjoy every day, even if it's just going to see a movie. Also, as I discussed earlier in this chapter, be sure to exercise daily. The natural endorphins you generate through exercise will help to ease the pain and give you energy to do more.

Don't Take It Out on Your Family

Finally, don't take it out on your family. You'll need them for support. Yes you're angry and want to let it out. Let it out but don't direct it toward a family member. Don't start yelling about actions taken by a family member that normally wouldn't even set you off. Keep close tabs on your anger and be sure you're not targeting others just to make it easier to let off steam.

RECAP: You may need longer than one week to complete the tasks in this chapter. Don't be discouraged if you need to take longer than a week, but before you move on to Chapter 3, be sure you:

- Memorize the steps of grieving and work through them.
- Learn the power of exercise and how it will help you.
- Discover ways to deal with your anger appropriately.
- Deal with your depression head on. You can't make a good impression on an interview until you do.
- Tell your family and friends about your layoff.
- Discover things you definitely should not do.

CHAPTER 3

Week 2: Lifestyles of the Temporarily Unemployed

THE SECOND WEEK after layoff you should be ready to start working on the rest of your life. The first order of business must be financial survival. Until you get that sorted out, there is no way you can focus on looking for a job. Nagging financial worries will kill any chance you have of focusing your needed efforts on the work ahead to find a new position.

First you'll need to take stock of what you have on hand, what cash flow you can expect until you find a new job, what you'll do about health and other benefits, what you'll do about your retirement savings and other assets related to your former job, and what you'll do about your debts. In this chapter we explore how to spend your second week getting your financial house in order, so you can focus on finding your next job.

Assess Your Financial Position

Before you can even think of developing a budget, you first need to assess the cash and cash equivalents (CDs, money market funds, stocks, bonds or anything else you can quickly turn into cash) you have on hand. Write down all the sources of cash you know you could access if needed while looking for work. Include the severance check you just got from your former employer, savings, nonretirement or education investment accounts, your spouse's salary (if you have a spouse who is working), and any future severance payments you might be expecting (for example, often a company will pay severance based on your former pay schedule).

Next make a list of people from whom you may be able to borrow money if needed. You may never end up borrowing this money, but putting it down on paper can give you some sense of security if it takes you longer than expected to find the job you want. You will only tap into these sources if absolutely needed, and they'll provide peace of mind so you don't panic about money in the short-term.

If you have a financial advisor, call him as soon as possible. He knows your financial position as well as you, if not better than you do. He can map out a financial plan to make you feel more confident about your financial situation so you can concentrate on the task at hand—finding a job.

Once you've pulled together your assets, add up your cash and known cash flow. On the following page is a chart you can use.

SOURCE	CASH ON HAND	FUTURE CASH	FLOW/ FREQUENCY
Severance Pay	$	$	/
Spouse's Pay	$	$	/
Unemployment Benefits	$	$	/
Checking Account	$	$	/
Savings Account	$	$	/
CD	$	$	/
Stocks	$	$	/
Bonds	$	$	/
Dividends	$	$	/
Interest	$	$	/
Royalties	$	$	/
Rental Income	$	$	/
Other	$	$	/
Total	$	$	/

Now you know what you have to work with immediately. Calculate all future cash flows as monthly payments, so you know how much more cash you will have to meet your bills on a monthly basis. If you have a three-month severance pay package, be sure to indicate the number of months that cash flow will be available as you calculate your future needs.

Unemployment Benefits

Don't forget to include your unemployment benefits in your financial worksheet. If you're entitled to benefits, claim them. If you think it's a hassle to enroll, or you think it's demeaning to stand in an unemployment line, get over it. Even if you're only able to collect $200 to $300 a week, this money will help you put food on the table and reduce your stress about finding work. It also will help ward off the need to ask for help from family or friends, which you probably find even more difficult.

Today, many states let you put in your initial application for unemployment online. Most let you report in weekly online or through a phone system. So don't expect that you'll need to go to an office and wait for hours. It's likely that won't be the case in your state. But, even if it is true, don't throw away benefits you deserve.

If you are getting severance based on your pay period, you may not be able to collect unemployment benefits until after the severance ends. Regardless, you should file an unemployment claim as soon as possible so your paperwork is in order and benefits will kick in when you need them. Be sure to review stipulations for state unemployment benefits online before calling or going down to the office.

Once you know what your unemployment benefit will be, when it starts and when it ends, add that to your assets worksheet. Unemployment benefits are a cash asset you can count on, so don't pass on the benefit just because you're embarrassed or harbor some other negative feelings toward them.

You may be wondering if you are eligible for unemployment. Each state has its own rules, but generally you must be unemployed through no fault of your own. A layoff definitely qualifies, but if you lost your job because of theft, insubordination, or frequent absences your company can contest your claim. If you were fired for poor performance or incompetence, you are still eligible to collect. If you resigned, your company likely will contest your claim to benefits unless you discussed this with them before you resigned. So if your company asks for volunteers to resign, don't step up unless you have another job lined up, because you will lose your rights to unemployment benefits. The one exception to this rule would be if your company offers a hefty severance package to those who resign and the package looks better to you than unemployment benefits.

Each state has its own rules regarding who is eligible for unemployment. Here's an overview of the key rules you're likely to find:

Your state will have rules regarding the minimum amount of time you must have a work history to collect unemployment. Many states require that you have a year of earnings on the books before you can collect.

You must be totally or partially unemployed. Sometimes you will qualify for some portion of weekly benefits if your work hours were cut because of lack of work.

You must have an approvable job separation. As I discussed above you could be disqualified for benefits if you were fired for certain reasons, which in unemployment doublespeak would be termed "fired for cause."

You must meet weekly legal requirements to qualify to collect benefits. You must guarantee that you were physically and mentally able to work, that you were seeking work, and you must file your weekly claim for benefits on a timely basis.

When you get to your state's unemployment office—many call them career centers or some happy euphemism that sounds better—be sure to check out whether they offer retraining programs. The state may pay for courses you need in order to get a new job, so research the program requirements while you are there.

One friend in New Jersey got the state to foot a large chunk of his bill to retrain in the computer field and secure professional certifications. This helped him land a great job with a much higher salary. So benefits offered by your state may not only be a weekly check. Be sure to ask about other services, such as career counseling and retraining.

Mortgage, Credit Cards, and Other Debts

After you've taken an inventory of your current and future cash availability, it's time to do the same type of inventory with your liabilities. Make a chart of all the money you pay out toward your debts and mandatory monthly bills. Here's a format that you can use:

ACCOUNT	MONTHLY PAYMENT
Mortgage or Rent	$
2nd Mortgage or Equity Line	$
Credit Card #1 *Minimum Payment*	$
Credit Card #2 *Minimum Payment*	$
Credit Card #3 *Minimum Payment*	$
Other Debts	$
Phone	$
Electric	$
Other Utilities	$
Water	$
Health Insurance	$
Total Bills	**$**

In addition to these bills, try to calculate what you spend on food and gas per month, so you'll be able to add that to the required budget.

Create a Budget

Now that you have a snapshot of your cash position, your monthly cash flow, and the amount of cash you need to pay your monthly mandatory bills, you can calculate how long you can stay afloat until you need a paycheck. Don't think of your severance as a windfall that you can spend all at once. Instead, be sure to include it in this monthly calculation. For example, if you got a three month severance package, don't continue spending as you did before your layoff. Figure a leaner budget so you can stretch your severance payment, which will give you more time to find a job without stressing about finances.

Calculate the amount you need to pay your mandatory bills each month. Now add to that your estimate for food and gas costs. This will give you your monthly "run rate"—the amount of money you need every month to pay for the basics of life.

Next, total your monthly cash flow. This will include your unemployment benefits, your spouse's income, your monthly severance, and any other cash you expect to come in every month.

Subtract the amount you need monthly to pay your mandatory bills. Is the answer a positive or negative number? To give you an idea of what this calculation might look like, let's look at the following example. Jack needs to pay out a total of $4,000 each month. His spouse earns $3,000 per month and he can count on $500 in unemployment for a total of $3,500 in income or money inflow. When you subtract $4,000 from $3,500, you get a total of minus $500. In other words, Jack's family will be $500 short each month to cover their basic monthly needs.

Next, let's take a look at how much you have in cash. In Jack's case, he got a lump sum severance payment of $5,000, but had no other savings. If his family can stay within that very tight budget he would have enough cash to cover the shortfall for ten months ($5,000/$500).

If he is unable to find a position within ten months, Jack will need to look at other sources for cash. And as his severance dwindles, Jack may want to take on a part-time job or consider contract work. The key for Jack, or anyone in this position, is to periodically run this type of analysis to see if he is able to stay within budget, tweak the budget numbers and run rate if necessary, and then project how long the remaining money will last. Once you find that you'll be out of cash in fewer than two months or so, it's time to find other sources for cash before you get into financial trouble.

When you complete this calculation you should be able to come to a similar conclusion about how much you may be short each month and how long your cash (or cash equivalent savings) will last. Taking the time to do this financial health check in Week 2 will help make the rest of your layoff less stressful because you'll have worked out a plan that reduces your fears of running out of money.

Ways to Raise Cash Quickly

If you have no liquid assets to count and you received only a one or two week severance, you may need to take other actions to start raising cash immediately so you can build up a cash cushion to make ends meet until you find a job. Speed is of the essence so you can avoid making late payments and destroying your credit.

Here are some ways to raise cash quickly:

Sell big items. Look at all your hard assets and figure out if there are some things you can sell for cash. Maybe you've kept an old car around just in case you need an extra one for your kids when they become teenagers. Sell the car and take the cash for now. Hopefully by the time your kids are ready to drive you'll have a great new job and will be able to afford to buy a new one. Even if that's not the case, you'll need to make the sacrifice for the good of the family. If you have a boat, electronics or other items you've been thinking of getting rid of, go for it. Advertise in a newspaper or online and sell them as soon as possible.

Organize a garage sale. Maybe you've been collecting stuff in your garage for a garage sale. Go ahead and get that done. You may not raise a lot of cash but every little bit will help and you will get your mind off the job loss for a little while as you plan and conduct the sale. A successful garage sale can also help you rebuild confidence in yourself and your abilities, so it can help your mood as well.

Turn your hobby into cash. Do you have something you've been doing on the side to help your neighbors and friends? For example, maybe you love woodworking and have been doing odd jobs, but haven't asked for cash. Let your friends know you're going to start a small business as a handyman, set up an hourly rate, and give out flyers or a business card to let your friends know you're available.

Find contract or freelance work. Do you have a particular skill you think businesses might need such as computer skills, bookkeeping skills, or writing and editing skills? You may be able to offer these skills to small businesses in the area and pick up some short-term contracts or freelance work. If you do a good job, this contract work could turn into your next job or could help expand contacts for networking.

Apply for new credit cards. If you got a sixty-day WARNing letter and have time to apply for new credit before you're let go, you may want to consider applying for some low-interest or zero interest credit cards that will give you access to quick cash for a year at almost no costs. You can search for the best twelve-month 0 percent or low percentage credit cards using the credit card tab at *www.bankrate.com*.

Apply for an equity line. If you have equity in your home and need cash that may also be a good source of some quick cash. But, be careful! When you take a loan against your

home's equity, you put your home at risk, especially if you
are unable to pay the mortgage at some point in the future.

When Your Cash Runs Dry

If you've exhausted all possible cash options that you're able
to raise on your own, you will have to make some hard choices.
You may find it very difficult to ask your mom and dad or your
grown children for money, but that option is a lot better than
destroying your credit. So if you have a source for cash that
might cause private embarrassment, swallow your pride and
ask for help.

Once you've exhausted all your options and are left with no
choice but to start skipping bill payments, call your creditors
and see what kind of deals you can work out with them. Many
won't even talk to you until you missed two payments, but it's
worth a try.

Call as soon as you realize you may miss a payment and
explain the situation. Some creditors may allow you to reduce
payments to interest-only payments until you get a new job.
Others may offer to lower your interest rate to help you through
a rough period. Still others may offer to add one or two payments to the back of your loan so you can skip a couple of payments without late notices and late fees.

Whether you've worked out an agreeable solution or not,
always make sure you get the name of the person you spoke
with and a way to call them back if there is a problem. Take
note of what was offered in detail, as well as the date and time
of the call, and ask to receive confirmation of the new offer
in writing. That way if there are any problems later you'll
have all the information you need to discuss what was offered
to you.

If you do need to miss payments for a few months while
you're looking for work and can't get your creditors to negoti-

ate, you're better off missing payments to credit card companies than to your mortgage company. Most credit cards are not secured against your home, but make sure that is the case. As long as a credit card is unsecured, you don't have to worry about losing your home if you don't pay the bills.

After a few months of nonpayments on your mortgage, your lender may start foreclosure proceedings. But, if you stay in touch with your lender, let them know the difficulties and that they are temporary, they probably will work with you on a payment plan or loan modification to help you stay in your home. The key is to be truthful with them and don't avoid making the calls. The U.S. Department of Housing and Urban Development (*www.hud.gov/foreclosure/index.cfm*) offers housing counselors and other tips to help you avoid foreclosure and stay in your home, so don't be afraid to ask for help. The sooner you ask the better.

If you've tried to work with your lenders and you can't seem to get them to work with you, don't give up. Instead, contact a nonprofit credit counseling agency. Note that many credit counselors don't act in the best interest of their clients and charge outrageous fees that make your credit situation worse not better. Your best bet is to find a credit counselor affiliated with the National Foundation for Credit Counselors (*www .nfcc.org*). You should seek help even before you miss any bills. They may be able to negotiate payment agreements to lower your monthly amount and/or lower your interest rate. You can reach them by calling 1-800-388 -2227. The folks who answer the national 800 number can help you find assistance closer to home.

Health and Other Benefits

As discussed in Chapter 2, you will be eligible for health insurance benefits through COBRA, but you may not be able to afford them. You will have to pay 100 percent plus a possible 2 percent administrative fee on top of that to continue your health benefits. That can run up to $800 a month or more for a family. Can you work your COBRA payments into your budget and still be able to pay your mortgage or rent, as well as pay for your food? Many families cannot. If you are married and your spouse's company offers health coverage for families, you should research how to get covered with his benefits.

Whether or not you continue your health benefits will depend on your individual situation. If your family is healthy with very little in medical costs you may decide to take the risk to work without medical insurance. That is a big risk and you could end up in bankruptcy if you or a member of your family is diagnosed with something major or is in a major accident soon after you give up your insurance.

If a family member is in the middle of cancer treatments or treatment for some other major illness, you will want to find a way to continue COBRA because you won't have a chance of getting any type of health insurance with that type of pre-existing condition. This means you might have to immediately find temporary work at a much lower salary so you can afford health insurance until you land in your next permanent position. As you interview for jobs, explain you took the work because you needed it to support your family. It won't be held against you.

If your family is generally healthy, you may be able to find insurance for a much cheaper monthly cost than COBRA. Be sure to carefully compare the benefits you are being offered and be sure you understand exactly how the new insurance works before you cancel COBRA. All individual insurance programs will have waiting periods, so if someone in your family has a chronic condition you may not have coverage for a twelve-month period and possibly longer in some states. Health insurance is regulated on a state-by-state basis.

Pension Funds and Stock Options

I purposely did not mention retirement savings or education savings accounts as part of your emergency cash stash, because that should definitely be your last option for tapping cash. Most retirement plans carry a 10 percent penalty if you take money out before you are fifty-nine-and-a-half years old. In addition to that you must pay taxes on what you take out based on your current tax rate.

For example, suppose you are earning enough to be in the 15 percent income tax bracket and you take out a lump sum that bumps you up to the 25 percent income tax bracket in total earnings for the year. Your employer would need to take out 35 percent in taxes from the lump sum you request.

Suppose you want to take out $50,000 in cash from your employer retirement savings account (such as a 401(k)). You would have to ask for $77,000 in order to get that amount in cash. Why so much? Because of that sum, $7,700 will go toward paying the penalty and $19,250 will go toward paying the income taxes due. In other words, $26,950 goes toward taxes and penalty, and $50,050 goes to you.

In addition to the taxes and penalty you must pay, you won't be able to replace that critical retirement savings in the future. Once you take it out, it's lost. Suppose instead you leave that savings in your retirement fund for ten years and are able to earn 8 percent on the mutual funds in which the money is invested. What will the $77,000 be worth? You will have more than $170,000.

Not only do you lose the savings you've built up for so many years with contributions from both you and your employer, you lose the continued growth of the money you'll need even more desperately in retirement when you can no longer work. So you may find it a quick and easy fix to take money out of your retirement accounts. But only look to do so if you truly have no other options to save your house. Be sure you've exhausted all your options, including selling something, doing temporary work, starting up a small business based on a hobby, or seeking help from family and friends.

What types of retirement accounts full under this umbrella of tax payments and penalties? Let's take a closer look at what they are and how they work.

401(k) and 403(b)

The 401(k) and 403(b) are the two most common retirement savings plans you'll find in the workplace. The name 401(k) and 403(b) actually represent parts of the tax code under which these programs were established. The 401(k) is offered by for profit companies and the 403(b) is offered by nonprofit organizations. In fact, if you work for a nonprofit you may not even realize you are part of a 403(b) because they tend to call them Tax-Sheltered Annuities (TSAs), Tax-Deferred Annuities (TDAs), or savings plans. For those of you who work for state government, your plan may be similar to the 403(b), but is called a Section 457.

The 401(k) and 403(b) retirement plans are also known as salary reduction plans. How do they work? Your salary is reduced by a percentage or dollar amount that you designate. The amount is deposited tax-deferred in a pension account in your name and it grows tax-free until retirement. Many employers match some portion of your contribution. A typical match is 50 percent of the first 6 percent contributed, but that varies greatly by company.

You may also hear these programs described as defined contribution plans. They differ greatly from defined benefit plans, which is the more traditional kind of employer-sponsored pension plan. defined contribution plans specify how much the employee and employer will contribute to the plan, while defined benefit plans specify the guaranteed benefit the employee can expect at retirement.

If you are laid off from a company with a defined benefit, whether or not you can withdraw the funds in a lump sum and how much that lump sum will be varies greatly. The withdrawal rules from a company with a defined benefit plan depend upon the pension documents and the formula set in those documents. If you were participating in a defined benefit plan, be sure to contact a financial advisor familiar with plans before making any decisions about withdrawing your money.

In this book I'm only going to take a closer look at how you withdraw funds from defined contribution plans. With these plans you can take out a lump sum and roll it over into an Individual Retirement Account (IRA). You can also decide *not* to roll it over, but based on the information I discussed above regarding taxes and penalties, as well as the loss of future gains, I strongly encourage you to avoid pulling these funds out for personal use after a layoff.

defined contribution plans give you more control over how the money is invested, but you also take more risk. If your investment choices are not sound, you may not have enough to receive the benefits you need at retirement. If you've followed the collapse of Enron, you probably saw stories about their employees losing over $850 million in their retirement savings because too much of their 401(k) assets were invested in company stock.

So if your 401(k) is primarily in company stock, you definitely want to change the mix. Your layoff could indicate signs of trouble at your company. Do you really want your retirement future banking on the success of this company? You're better off taking the money out. Financial advisors recommend that no more than 15 percent of your retirement assets be held in the stock of the company for which you work. That amount should drop to no more than 4 percent after you leave the company.

How much you'll get to take out will depend on the provisions of your company's Defined Contribution Plan. If your company has made contributions, you may not be able to take out all of those contributions; some may go back into the company's coffers. This will depend on what's called "vesting."

Vesting

Vesting rules specify how long you must participate in a company's retirement plan before you get to keep 100 percent of the company's contributions to the plan. If you are laid off before you are 100 percent vested in the company you may lose some of the money the company deposited in your 401(k) or 403(b) account. You don't have to worry about the money you put into the plan. That is 100 percent vested from the day you put it in. There are two types of vesting rules allowed by the government "graded" and "cliff" vesting. Here's how those work:

Graded Vesting. Employees become vested in 20 percent of their accrued benefits after an initial period of service (usually one or three years). Then each year after that first year, you become invested in an additional 20 percent with full vesting four years later. The length of the initial period of vesting depends on how your employer determines the amount of contributions. If your employer uses a fixed percentage of your contribution, then the initial period of service can be no longer than two years. If the employer's contribution is a set amount not related to your contribution, then the initial period of service can be as long as three years with full vesting after seven years of service.

Cliff Vesting. Employees remain unvested during their initial period of service but become fully vested after that. So if you're company uses this type of vesting, you'll get none of the employer's contribution if you are laid off before being fully vested. The initial period of service required depends on how your employer determines the amount of its contribution. If your employer's contribution is a fixed amount of your salary, the initial service required can be no more than three years. If the employer's contribution is a set amount without regard to your contribution than the initial service period can be no more than five years.

The rules I've stated here are the maximum number of years allowed by the government. Your company can decide to fully vest you sooner, but very few do. If your employer imposes a two-year waiting period before you are eligible for the company match, then company contributions must be fully vested immediately upon becoming eligible. If your employer retirement savings plan was terminated before you were laid off, then all participants in the plan become 100 percent vested immediately and you won't lose any of your employer's matched contributions.

If you are laid off, your best bet is to roll the money in your 401(k) or 403(b) into an IRA because then you will have full control over how your money is invested. If you leave it with your employer, you can only choose among the investments offered by your employer. Many times you can find mutual fund families with a broad selection of funds available with lower management fees and no up-front commission charges (no-load), such as Vanguard, Fidelity or T. Rowe Price.

Be sure you roll your funds into an existing account with a mutual fund company, bank or brokerage. Don't ask for a check from your employer and then deposit it into an account. In fact, in most cases the company that will be accepting the funds will help you with the roll-over process. The reason I give you this warning is that the government allows you to hold onto the funds for only sixty days. If you hold the funds for sixty-one days or more you will be hit with the taxes and penalties I mentioned above. By rolling the funds directly into another account you don't risk any problems with government. You also won't be tempted to spend the money. If you do spend the money without setting aside the taxes and penalties, you may need to take a loan to pay them later.

While most large employers and some small employers offer 401(k) or 403(b) plans, some smaller employers offer something called a SIMPLE IRA. Let's take a quick look at how that works.

Simple IRA

Another retirement plan alternative for small businesses is the SIMPLE IRA. It was designed by Congress to give small businesses an alternative that would be easier and less costly to administer than the 401(k).

The SIMPLE IRA gives small businesses the opportunity to offer a tax-deferred salary reduction plan similar to a 401(k), but without the extensive administrative costs a 401(k) plan can incur. Employees can elect to make contributions up to $10,500 in 2007 ($13,00 if the employee is fifty years or older), which is indexed to inflation each year.

Employers must match the employee contribution dollar for dollar up to three percent of the employee's compensation. If you are over fifty you can make additional catch-up contributions of $1,000 in 2007. The amount of catch-up contributions allowed will be indexed to inflation.

In addition to the requirement for company matching provisions, the rules for transferring SIMPLE IRAs if you change jobs are much stricter. Your SIMPLE IRA account must be open for at least two years before you can transfer the money. If you want to move your money before the two-year period has ended, there is a 25 percent tax penalty whether you withdraw or transfer it to another retirement plan. If you do switch jobs before the two-year period is up, it is best to leave the money in the SIMPLE IRA. The money is in your name. The only reason to take a 25 percent tax penalty hit would be if you thought the financial institution holding the money was at risk of losing it all. Once the two-year period is up, you do have the choice to roll the money into another IRA or into your new company's 401(k).

Deferred Profit-Sharing Plans

Small business employers can supplement any of their retirement plans with a deferred profit-sharing plan (DPSP). Employers can contribute up to 18 percent of an employee's compensation up to $10,500 in 2008 and $11,000 in 2009. Starting in 2010 this will be indexed for inflation.

Employers who offer this type of plan do so primarily to give employees a stake in the business by sharing company profits. They are considered a good way to encourage higher efficiency and increase morale and the hope is that they will result in higher profits. These plans can also help in employee retention. Vesting provisions keep employees around if they want their money. When you are laid off, be sure your severance package includes information about what will happen with your share of the DPSP plan.

DPSP offer employers a lot of flexibility in how they plan their contributions, so they can better match according to business conditions each year. Employer contributions are exempt from federal payroll taxes, which help to offset plan costs. Employers do not have to provide a definite formula for figuring the profits to be shared, but if there isn't a formula they must make systematic and substantial contributions.

Employers must develop a definite formula for allocating the contribution among the participants and for distributing the accumulated funds to employees, such as after they reach a certain age or after a fixed number of years. If employees forfeit their profit-sharing funds because they leave the company before being vested, the forfeitures can be allocated among the remaining employees or can be used to reduce future contributions.

Ways to Withdraw Retirement Funds Without Penalty

You can avoid penalties for withdrawing retirement funds from an IRA, but you will still have to pay taxes on the money you take out at your current income tax rate, if:

You want to buy a house for the first time. You can withdraw up to $10,000 penalty free.

You want to pay for qualified education expenses for you, your spouse, your kids, or even your grandkids. Expenses that qualify include post-secondary school education, tuition, books, supplies, room, and board. Room and board is only eligible if the student is enrolled at least half-time.

You become disabled and qualify for a disability exemption. You must prove that you are incapable of working.

You have medical expenses that need to be reimbursed. Expenses must exceed 7.5 percent of your adjusted gross income.

You must pay for your health insurance out of pocket because you become unemployed. You can only begin withdrawing these funds after twelve consecutive weeks of collecting unemployment benefits.

Attention, Older Workers

If you are laid off at age fifty-five or anytime before the age of fifty-nine and a half, you'll find special rules that allow you to withdraw funds before fifty-nine and a half without incurring a penalty. If you participate in a 401(k), the Internal Revenue Code Section 71(t) states that any employee "separated from service" (laid off, fired, or resigned) and who is at least age fifty-five in the year in which this occurs, may take distributions from his employer-sponsored retirement plan without incurring the 10 percent penalty. You will still owe income tax on any money that is withdrawn.

Another option is to annuitize an IRA if you are five years away from the allowable age for withdrawal—fifty-nine and a half. To take advantage of this rule you would take annual cash withdrawals based on your life expectancy, as predicted by the IRS. If you want to take advantage of this rule, get the charts for annuitizing an IRA from the IRS or contact your tax advisor to help you figure out how to do this.

For example, suppose you have $100,000 in your IRA and the IRS actuarial tables predict you will live for twenty more years. You can then withdraw one-twentieth of the balance in your account for the first year or $2,000 without penalty. You would have to pay income taxes at your current income tax rate though. Then the next year you would withdraw one-nineteenth of your balance. The third year, one-eighteenth of your balance.

If you were fifty-five when you started, in the fourth year you'd be turning fifty-nine and a half and then there are no restrictions on withdrawals, but be careful because you will still need to pay income taxes on the money you take out. If you take a big lump in one year you could end up pushing yourself into a higher tax bracket and be surprised by the size of your tax bill.

It's Not All about the Money

I've talked a lot about getting your financial cards in order, but it's not only about money. You're lifestyle has changed. Your family members were used to having you out of the house and they were able to follow their own routines. You're upsetting the apple cart by being home more often.

This week, be mindful of that and be careful not to step where you may not be wanted. Give your family a chance to move on as they were before and watch what goes on. Get involved if you can help, but don't fight it if a family member pushes back. If your spouse works full time, offer to take on more of the responsibility around the house and work out a to-do list that you both agree is acceptable.

I've heard some people say that looking for a job is harder than a nine-to-five job, and while that's true, it doesn't mean that you will actually be pounding the pavement from nine to five each day. Most people can work effectively at looking for work for about four hours a day. What are you going to do with the rest of that time? Volunteering and getting yourself out of the house is definitely a good option, but making life easier for the rest of your family will also go a long way toward alleviating the tension everyone is feeling about your job loss.

RECAP: You may need longer than one week to complete the tasks in this chapter. Don't be discouraged if you need to take longer than a week, but before you move on to Chapter 4, be sure you:

- Assess your financial position and establish a financial foundation.
- Develop a budget that matches the cash you now have available each month.
- Know how or where you can raise additional cash if needed.
- Deal with your health care coverage.
- Determine what you will do with any pension or retirement savings.
- Prepare yourself for the lifestyle change.

• Reassessing your skills and interests
• Re-evaluating your career
• Next steps

CHAPTER 4

Week 3: There's Life After a Layoff

ONCE YOU GET your finances in order, it's time to focus on what you want to do next. Do you want to stay in the same industry or are you ready to move on to something else? In this chapter, we explore those questions and then focus on the next steps you'll need to take to turn your layoff into an opportunity to improve your work situation.

Life Inventory

Before you move on you should take the time to look back over your previous job as well as your career. You don't need to spend a lot of time on this, maybe just a few hours to determine what happened and ask yourself if you could have done anything differently to change the outcome. You will need to be honest with yourself and if you are you may find some strengths and weaknesses that will help you be more successful on your next job. You want to think of ways to overcome the weaknesses and ways to build on your strengths.

Listing Your Strengths, Weaknesses, and Passions

Let's take some time to discover your strengths, weaknesses, and passions. This will help you make better job choices in the future. Most people find it difficult to admit that they have weaknesses. You'll need to get over that if you want to help yourself now. Be honest. No one will see what you write down now unless you chose to show it to them, so do your best at searching within yourself for both your strengths and your weaknesses.

First, let's do some brainstorming. Write down everything that you are really good at or that you really enjoy doing. We're brainstorming now so don't worry about whether you can actually find a job doing what you enjoy. Just write down what you think are your strongest skills and your true passions.

Doing this will help you find a job that builds on your strengths. By knowing your weaknesses, you can avoid a job that you think will accent those and therefore lead to yet another failure. Also it will be much easier to show up at the workplace everyday.

If you're having a hard time putting together this list, I find one of the best ways to figure out what I want to do next is to make a list of what I liked doing best at my previous jobs. Next I make a list of what I liked least. Having a hard time putting together that list? It doesn't have to only include tasks that were part of your job. Suppose you really enjoy helping others figure out their personal finances. If that's the case, a good job for you may be something in the financial industry. You may need to take some courses first, but you might be much happier with that type of job. Or, suppose you like helping friends decorate their homes. Maybe you would enjoy training to become an interior decorator or to work as a salesperson or design consultant for a developer.

Now that you are out of work you can totally reinvent yourself or you can continue along the same career path. It's up to you. If you loved your job, then you probably want to seek work in the same or similar industry. If you hated your job, use this opportunity to change your life by changing what you do.

A NEW PATH

After each of my layoffs I took time to reassess my skills and what I liked to do, and I changed directions dramatically after each layoff. When I was laid off from a position of communications coordinator for a small nonprofit university center, one of my close friends encouraged me to try real estate sales. She thought I was an excellent communicator and could do well. I ended up working in new homes sales for eight years until I decided to go back and get my MBA.

After I got my MBA, I went to work for a major university center doing fundraising until I was laid off from that position and then I reinvented myself again. I decided I wanted to start rebuilding my writing career, but this time as a financial writer. I took a management job for a few years to build up my savings but I also built my writing reputation at the same time. I then took a job as content director for a new dot-com start-up. When I was laid off from the dot-com, I finally launched the writing business I'm still doing today. By taking time to take inventory of my life, skills, and interests, I was able to create my own path and land in a career that is satisfying. Do yourself a favor and take that time to truly assess yourself.

Self-Assessment

So how do you get started? One helpful tool to assist you with deciding what to do next is to discover your worker type. You can try some of the formal online self-assessment tests noted below or you can take tests working with a professional counselor (more that later in the chapter), but first let's see how much you can figure out on your own. Maybe you'll feel confident enough about your self-assessment that you won't need to spend the money on tests or on a counselor.

We'll begin by sorting out the type of worker you are, as well as identifying the type of work that might fit you the best.

To do this, try this common personality test. Quickly circle eight words or phrases in the table below that best fit your image of yourself. Do this quickly. The quicker the better if you want to get answers that truly match your personality. The longer you think about it, the less instinctive your answers will be. Also don't cheat by looking at the explanations below this table or you'll diminish the value of this exercise. Pick eight words or phrases from the list below that best describe your personality:

WORD	VALUE	WORD	VALUE
Adventurous	E	Mechanically inclined	R
Analytical	I	Methodical	C
Assertive	E	Nature Lover	R
Athletic	R	Numerically inclined	C
Broad-minded	I	Obedient	C
Concrete	R	Observant	I
Conforming	C	Open	A
Conscientious	C	Optimistic	E
Cooperative	S	Orderly	C
Creative	A	Outgoing	S
Efficient	C	Patient	S
Empathetic	S	Precise	I
Energetic	E	Scholarly	I
Expressive	A	Scientific	I

Word	Value	Word	Value
Extroverted	E	Self-confident	E
Forgiving	S	Self-controlled	R
Friendly	S	Sensitive	S
Generous	S	Spontaneous	E
Helpful	S	Stable	R
Imaginative	A	Straightforward/frank	R
Innovative	S	Structured	C
Intellectually self-confident	I	Talkative	E
Intuitive	S	Unconventional	A
Logical	I	Well-organized	C

Once you've finished circling the words or phrases add up how many of each letter value you have:

As	_____
Cs	_____
Es	_____
Is	_____
Rs	_____
Ss	_____

As you look at your totals, you will probably find that you have one dominant value of three or more and several of one or two. The dominant value represents your strongest worker type. But don't count out the other values. They too influence what you like to do.

Please see Value Definitions on page 74

Let's look at what these values mean:

A = Artistic (also known as Creators)
C = Conventional (also known as Organizers)
E = Enterprising (also known as Persuaders)
I = Investigative (also known as Thinkers)
R = Realistic (also known as Doers)
S = Social (also known as Helpers)

Now let's look at the strengths of each of these worker types and what they like to do most. Then we'll look at some sample job choices that best fit each worker type. You may find some ideas for your next job after you read this section if you did the test quickly without looking at the answers first.

Artistic (Creators)

If you fit into this worker type, you probably excel in one of the following areas: acting; dance; art; fashion or interior design; or music. You may enjoy attending concerts; going to theater; visiting art exhibits; reading fiction, plays or poetry; taking photographs; working on crafts; and expressing yourself in other creative ways. If you're this type of worker you're good at dealing with ambiguous ideas, so you don't need to take a job where everything is given to you clearly in black and white. In fact you might hate that type of job.

Since you're artistic, your passion or hobby may be easily turned into a business for profit. For example, if any of the following hobbies match your personal skills, you may be able to turn them into a successful small business: designing sets for plays, desktop publishing, homemade crafts, painting, photography, sewing, or writing. You may enjoy other artistic hobbies, but they probably won't help you make any extra money, such as taking dance lessons, playing a musical instrument, or traveling.

If you're an artistic type, the best jobs for you may be copywriter, drama or English teacher, editor, graphic or interior designer, photographer, or writer.

Conventional (Organizers)

People with a conventional worker-type personality tend to work best within a well-defined system and can do a lot of paperwork in a short time. If you're a conventional worker type, you also probably excel at keeping accurate records, entering data into a computer, or writing effective business letters. You're likely to prefer working within clearly defined processes, enjoy using data processing equipment, like working with numbers, excel at keeping track of details, and enjoy collecting or organizing.

Hobbies you might enjoy include collecting memorabilia, playing computer or card games, keeping club or family records and files, reading home magazines, and writing your family history. You won't find that any of these hobbies translate easily into a small business, but your strong organizational skills might give you some options to assist other small businesses with record keeping, bookkeeping, or other organizational needs. So you may be able to generate some part-time or temporary work while you look for another job.

If you don't already have coursework in accounting, you may want to take some time and get credentials so you can work as an accountant or bookkeeper. Other types of jobs you may enjoy include bank teller, cashier, clerk, data processor, or librarian.

Enterprising (Persuaders)

If you are an enterprising worker type, you may like to initiate projects and convince people to do things your way. You probably enjoy selling things, promoting ideas, or persuading others to follow your lead. You most likely enjoy giving speeches or leading a group. You're probably also good at organizing activities and persuading others to join you.

You probably look to build power or status and enjoy wining a leadership or sales award. Your first choice may be to start your own business or campaign for someone else in a political campaign. Your hobbies are likely to include discussing politics, reading business journals, watching the stock market, attending meetings and conferences, and leading community organizations.

With these skills when it comes to finding a new job, you might want to consider work as a bartender, financial planner, international interpreter, lobbyist, manufacturer's representative, public relations representative, real estate agent, salesperson, or travel agent.

Investigative (Thinkers)

If your primary worker type is investigative, then you likely excel at thinking abstractly, solving mathematical problems, or understanding scientific theories. Things you enjoy probably include doing complex calculations, interpreting formulas, and using a microscope or computer. You likely prefer to work independently, using computers or working in a lab doing experiments.

In addition you may enjoy analyzing data, doing research, or reading scientific or technical journals to challenge your intellect. Your hobbies might include joining a book club, collecting things (such as rocks, stamps or coins), doing crossword puzzles, or studying astronomy. You also might enjoy getting involved in conservation efforts or working to save an endangered species.

If you have these skills, you may want to consider jobs that include management consultant, medical lab technologist, or research analyst, science teacher or technical writer. If you have strong computer skills, you may want to consider IT work as well.

Realistic (Doers)

Realistic workers like to repair things. You likely enjoy operating tools and machinery, reading blueprints, or solving electrical problems. For fun you might enjoy camping or you might like to play sports or maybe you enjoy planting a garden. You probably find that your first preferences are to work outdoors and work with your hands. You probably look for things to do that will allow you to be physically active or build things.

Your hobbies might include building models, coaching team sports, growing plants and flowers, hunting and fishing, landscaping, playing sports, refinishing furniture, repairing cars or other equipment, target shooting, and woodworking. You may be able to make extra money doing things for others while you look for a job or you may want to use your talents to start a new business.

Jobs you may want to consider include automobile mechanic, carpenter, electrician, groundskeeper, painter, or plumber.

Social (Helpers)

Helpers enjoy teaching or training others. If you are a social type, you likely are good at expressing yourself clearly and breaking things down into smaller pieces, so it's easier for others to learn. You probably enjoy leading a support group or mediating a dispute. You likely work well with others and enjoy planning or supervising activities.

These skills make you good at helping people solve their problems. You probably like working with young people or maybe you enjoy caring for children. Your hobbies likely include helping others with personal concerns, joining community organizations, and volunteering in social action groups. You're very gregarious and like to meet new friends, go to parties, or play in team sports. You may be active in a religious organization.

When it comes to looking for work, you may want to consider jobs as a counselor, librarian, mediator, real estate appraiser, social worker, or teacher.

Using Your Worker Type to Decide Next Steps

After figuring out your worker type, you will have even more information to help you sort out your strengths and weaknesses. If you've been having a hard time determining what you like to do and what you don't like to do, this exercise should give you some insights into that as well.

You may have found that your personality actually fits into several worker type categories. Search inside yourself to tease out the dominant type or mix and match your skill sets to understand what to look for in your next job.

Your Work Style

Finding out your worker type is not the only important part of this decision. You also must consider how you like to work. You may enjoy working by yourself or you may prefer working as a team. Some people prefer to work with a lot of direction, while others prefer to work without a supervisor looking over their work all the time. Think about what's true for you, because if you end up in a work environment that doesn't match your working style, you won't be happy with the job and probably won't succeed.

Autonomous Workers

If you like to work autonomously, look for a job that will allow you to work by yourself without much supervision. If you don't, you'll spend most of your day resenting your supervisor and creating a lot of tension.

If you don't like regular supervision, do yourself a favor and don't accept that type of job. Talk about your preference to work autonomously during your interview, so if the person hiring you knows he prefers control over your work he won't hire you.

If this discussion does create a problem during the interview, you probably don't want the job anyway. You'd end up butting heads with someone who prefers to keep a tight reign on his or her staff and lose the job quickly. Don't push it if you and your potential employer have different working styles. Your best bet is to move on and look for something else.

Direction Seekers

You're someone who prefers lots of direction and clear instructions. You probably don't like to make decisions. If this is true for you, then look for a job in which the supervisor prefers to be in control and gives you direction. Be sure to let the interviewer know that you prefer a work situation that is clearly defined with duties clearly spelled out, so you know what is expected of you. If you don't, you could end up in a job with a company that doesn't define roles and expects people to just jump and do whatever is necessary without much direction.

Team Players

You may prefer to work in teams rather than on your own. If that is your preference, target companies that encourage teamwork. In today's world that is probably the most common theme for most businesses, so you shouldn't have a hard time finding a job where teamwork is the norm.

Matching Skills and Jobs

Now that you've uncovered your worker types and pre-ferred worker style, let's take a look at how you can use these ideas to find jobs that might interest you. You may be wondering if you have all the skills for the job. One of the best ways to research skill sets is to use a tool online at CareerOneStop (*www.careeronestop.com*).

To use the career skills profiler at CareerOneStop, go to *www.acinet.org/acinet/skills*. Using the tool, you can get a comprehensive list of the skills you need for just about any job. You can start the search in one of two ways—by searching or browsing job type or by focusing on job skills.

If you know that you want to work in a particular field, but aren't sure exactly what you want to do in that field, you can find a job type by searching job types. For example, if you know you'd like to work in the financial field, but are not sure what type of job you want, then you would use the use the "Browse by Job Type" option. If you want to look at various job types, then use the "Browse Jobs" option.

Once you've completed the search using either of these methods and get your skills profile, you will see a list of occupations that match your profile. Click on any occupation listed to find a comprehensive overview of the particular occupation on a state-by-state basis. This overview will include wages that can be expected, job trends nationwide and in your state, a list of the most important knowledge, skills, and abilities for the occupation you've chosen, the education and training you need, and any related occupation profiles. Also, once you've completed the skills profiler, you can select to compare your skills to the skills needed for occupations that interest you.

What Do You *Really* Want To Do?

After taking these simple tests and using the CareerOneStop tool, you still may not be sure what you'd like to do. You don't have to figure that out alone. You may want to try counseling services or career testing opportunities.

Finding a Professional Career Counselor

If you feel as if you have exhausted all the help you can get out of your family and friends, but still can't decide what to do next, it's time to look elsewhere. Sometimes you need to find a dispassionate third party that can help you sort through your choices and dig into your psyche to help you find what's best for you.

SEARCH SMART

After a layoff you have the opportunity to take an entirely new path. You may not have searched for a job in quite some time. Maybe the job market is much different than when you first got out of school or a lot different from the last time you searched for work. You need to:

Take the time to plan a path that fits your personal values, interests, likes, dislikes, and skill levels at this phase of your life. You'll probably find that these values, interests, likes, and dislikes are much different than they were when you left school.

Take the time to define exactly what you want from your next job. For example, your last job may have been one where you worked nearly 24/7 and you'd like to find something that gives you more time to spend with your family. You may not want another highly stressful and demanding job. A career counselor can help you sort that out.

Set goals and deadlines for yourself that are realistic and will help you find your next job. A third party who is not emotionally impacted by the job loss might help you be more realistic based on the current job market.

Don't be concerned if you seem as undecided as you were when you first graduated high school or entered college. You've lost your job and are entering a new phase of life. Don't think that there is something wrong with you just because you need a little help.

Career counseling involves much more than just figuring out what you want to do when you get out of school. You might be having trouble even getting out of bed. A counselor can help you set up a routine that will make your job search more effective. Career counselors frequently work with older adults to sort out career and life planning issues. No matter your age, these changes are huge for anyone and getting help from a professional can make this transition much easier for you. A professional can also help you make the right choices that will lead to a job that you enjoy and that fits your personality.

So, how do you go about looking for a job counselor? One of the best ways to find a good counselor is to seek references from friends, associates, or possibly the human resources staff at your former company. If you don't know anyone who can recommend someone, a good place to start is the National Board of Certified Counselors (*www.nbcc.org/counselorfind2*).

Once you do find a number of counselors, how do you choose the one that is right for you? Interview the counselors and ask key questions, such as "How much experience do you have working with adults at or near my age group?" You definitely want to find a counselor who has experience working with someone at or near your age group. For example, someone who is thirty years old and near the beginning of his career will face significantly different issues than someone who is fifty years old with lots of work experience.

You also should make sure you connect with the counselor personally. If you don't feel comfortable talking with the counselor, you won't be able to work together and you won't get the help you need. If you do think the counselor is a good match for you, don't forget to ask for referrals. You certainly don't want to pay someone who is merely a smooth talker.

Services of career counselors differ depending on the counselor's level of experience and the types of clients with whom the counselor works. When you are looking for a counselor you need to find one that focuses on whole-life career planning. Be sure to ask about a counselor's credentials, clientele, testing, scope, and outcomes.

CAREER COUNSELOR DUE DILIGENCE

Credentials—Career counselors don't have to be licensed in most states, so anyone who is self-trained can hang out a shingle. Ask where the counselor trained, whether she has an advanced degree in psychology or social work, and whether she's sought certification from a professional group, such as the National Board of Certified Counselors or the National Career Development Association.

Clientele—Ask the counselor whether she specializes in certain types of clients, such as those beginning careers, those finding jobs after a layoff, or those near retirement or transitioning to retirement. You definitely want to find a counselor who works with clientele near your age group or with similar career issues.

Testing—Ask what type of testing is used as part of the process. Does she assess career change and transferable skills? Does she provide an interpretation of test results?

Scope—Ask about the counselor's scope. Can she help you not only with decisions related to your job choice, but also how that choice impacts this period of change, such as any personal barriers, family roles, and changing values? For example, in the past, career advancement may have been your priority, but now your primary goal may be to make enough money to support your family but not to have as much stress or travel as much as in past jobs so you can spend more time with family.

Outcomes—Ask how the counselor can help you discover your next steps. What can you expect will be the outcome of your work with the counselor?

Be sure you ask the counselors you are considering for a detailed explanation of their services. Make sure you understand the services being offered, their expectations about your degree of involvement, and your financial commitment.

When you choose a professional be sure to pick one who understands your career is a part of your life, so he will carefully consider your values as you start your next life adventure. You want a counselor who can help put your decision-making process in perspective—considering all your life choices, not just those related to work.

Talking with Your Counselor

Once you've found the right person, you're probably wondering what you should talk about and how the process will work. Many counselors will start by giving you a series of assessment tests, while others prefer to talk with you once or twice to get to know you before testing. Your career counselor likely will do one or more of the following:

- Invite you to participate in individual and group counseling sessions to help you clarify your life and career goals.
- Help you identify your options by administering and interpreting tests and inventories to assess your abilities, interests, values, and personality.
- Encourage you to explore your options through activities and planning experiences.
- Help you improve your decision-making skills.
- Help you relearn job hunting strategies (you may not have looked for a job in a long time) and assist with the development of a resume.

Testing to Assist Your Life and Career Choices

Whether or not you decide to work with a career counselor, you still may want to take some tests to get a better handle on your values, your interests, your personality, and your skills. If you've gotten to this point of the chapter and still have no idea what you want to do next, take the tests.

You probably haven't taken career tests since you left school. You may have taken them as you were trying to figure out what you wanted to do for the rest of your life, while you were in high school or college. You may be wondering why you should take any more of these tests now. You will find the way you answer the questions on these tests differs at different points of your life, depending on the type of decisions you are trying to make and how these decisions will impact your life planning. After you have a set of career experiences, your perspective changes and you may find you need to change your career path based on what you find out on these tests.

If you're someone who is nervous about taking tests, calm down! Don't think of these as tests for which you will be judged. You should instead think of them as tools for helping you make a decision. Don't expect these tests to find the perfect job for you or to map out your next steps. These tools will help you explore yourself. They will give you an opportunity to look at yourself in a type of intellectual mirror and help you determine what you might want to do next.

We will explore tests you can take online for free or for a small fee. If you do seek professional counseling, your counselor may give you similar tests as part of the counseling process.

Finding Out More About Your Values

You explore your values by taking inventories that measure what motivates you and how important different values are to you. These can include autonomy, flexible work schedule, helping others, interpersonal relations, leisure time, outdoor work, prestige, salary, and security. You may have found it hard to make a list of what you like and don't like from past work experiences, as I recommended earlier. Value inventories help you determine that. Here are three good ones available online:

The Values Questionnaire: (*www.morris.umn.edu/services/career/ career_planning/valquestion.php*) from the University of Minnesota assists you with exploring the things most important to you at this point of your life.

Soul Survival: Career Values: (*www.career-intelligence.com/ assessment/career_values.html*) from the website Career-Intelligence explains the importance of determining your values and then includes an accompanying exercise to help you do just that. You'll find lots of useful resources on this site.

Work-Related Values Assessment: (*http://cehd.umn.edu/ETCS/ career/ValuesSelfAssessment.pdf*), which was developed by the U.S. Department of Labor, can be found online at the University of Minnesota. This worksheet defines each of the core work values. Armed with this information, you are then asked to pick your three most important values.

Narrowing Down Your Interests

Narrowing down your interests can be a hard thing to do for some; for others it can be difficult to even list their interests. Interest inventories help you by asking questions regarding what activities you like to do and what activities you don't like to do. Determining these likes and dislikes can get you on the path of finding work you might enjoy.

Since online career interest inventories aren't free, don't bother with them if you're clear about your interests. But if want to delve deeper, or are still fuzzy about your interests, here are two good online inventories that you can use for a small fee:

The Campbell Interest and Skill Survey: (*www.pearsonassessments .com/tests/ciss.htm*) Formerly only available to career counselors, this is now available online for an $18 fee. It was developed by internationally recognized career expert, David Campbell and is published by NCS Pearson. This is a 320-question survey and your results are compared to those of people who are successfully employed in your fields of interest.

Self-Directed Search: (*www.self-directed-search.com*) Popular among career counselors, this fifteen-minute interest and skills assessment can be taken online for $9.95. Your report will appear on-screen once you've paid for the assessment. Before taking the test you can quickly review the format, including questions about your likes and dislikes of various activities, your competencies, your occupations, as well as take a self-assessment of your abilities.

Exploring Your Personality

Almost everyone wonders what people think of them. You may take the attitude that you don't care, but that's not a good answer. The type of impression you make during an interview can be based on that personality (unless you are a great actor or actress), so it's good to know as much about your personality as possible before you start looking for a job. Knowing your personality can help you find the right job and the right people with which to work.

You'll find that many personality inventories are based on the theories of psychologist Carl Jung. He believed that people were either extroverts or introverts and that there were six personality types: feeling, intuitive, judging, sensing, perceptive, and thinking. Basically, what these inventories do is sort out the ways people prefer to take in information and make decisions. They also look at how you get your energy—from the outside world or your inner self. Finally, they assess whether you are the type of person who likes to find closure or a person who prefers to keep options open.

You won't be able to find these tests for free either. In fact, the most respected personality test—the Myers-Briggs Type Indicator (MBTI)—requires that you pay for the interpretive assistance of a certified MBTI practitioner. How much you pay will be determined by the type of test you take (online or on paper) and the amount of counseling time involved. You can find sources for the test online at *www.career-intelligence.com*.

I don't recommend you take this test online. If you do think you need an extensive personality profiler, then your best bet is to work with a counselor, since you'll need to have the results interpreted by a professional and they will be more meaningful if done by someone who knows you.

However, if you are thinking of opening your own business, Career Intelligence offers a good package that includes the MBTI and the Strong Interest Inventory with a focus on whether you would do well opening your own business. This assessment will help you determine whether your personality and your interest fit the role of a small business owner. Interpretive counseling is also included in this package which is called, "Strong and MBTI Entrepreneur Report" (*www.career-intelligence.com/assessment/Entrepreneur.asp*). The fee for the package is $149.95.

One online test you can take that is similar to the MBTI, but much cheaper, is the Keirsey Temperament Sorter (*www.advisor team.com/temperament_sorter*), which is used by corporations, professional counselors, and major universities. After answering the seventy questions in this test you'll get insights into your temperament, personality types, and your motivations.

Assessing Your Skills

You may have found that it is very hard for you to list all your skills. In fact, even if you think you've made a good list of your skill set, you probably haven't. You may have worked for many years and done many different jobs during your lifetime. Many people overlook all the things they've learned over a lifetime of work. Don't despair! There are a number of skill profilers that can help you put together a list of your skills. Here are three good free online resources that can help you construct your skill profile:

Career One Stop Skills Profiler: (*www.acinet.org/acinet/skills*) Again, this excellent tool helps you not only to get a comprehensive list of your skills, but also helps you find career options that match those skills.

Career-Intelligence Skills Worksheet: (*www.career-intelligence .com*) This site offers an excellent article about how to develop your career skills set and a worksheet to help you do just that. You can access the article at *www.career-intelligence .com/assessment/career_skillset.asp* and the worksheet at *www .career-intelligence.com/assessment/career_skillset_worksheet.asp*. You will have to register for the site, but registration is free. Here you will find a series of exercises to help you sort out your skills. You'll find several different skill surveys you can complete.

Are You Ready for Your Job Search?

So now are you ready to start looking for a job? Can you honestly say that you've got enough distance from the layoff to make a good impression while networking with others or facing a job interview? Can you talk about your layoff in a way that makes you look good?

If you can't answer yes to these questions you're not ready to look for a job. You don't want to look for work too soon and make a bad first impression. You likely won't get a second chance if your first approach is done at a time when you're not psychologically ready.

Practice with family and friends and let them tell you what they think of your layoff story and how you tell it. If they don't like it, I can just about guarantee you a person who doesn't know you won't either. Let your family and friends help you develop an effective way to tell your layoff story, as well as help you get in a better frame of mind to tell it.

If, after the third week you're still harboring a lot of anger or just don't have a clear idea of what you want to do, don't rush your job search. Instead, do things that make you feel better. Maybe it's helping at your son's boy scout troop or volunteering at your church or synagogue. Or maybe it's volunteering at a national park near you. The one thing you definitely should avoid is moping around the house or staying in bed. I can guarantee you that won't get you into a better frame of mind for your job search.

As long as you're working on getting into a better frame of mind for your job search, you're looking for a job. You never know, maybe you'll meet just the right person for your network wherever you decide to volunteer your time and that person will introduce you to your next boss. It happens all the time. I've gotten three different permanent positions through contacts I've made volunteering with nonprofit organizations during my lifetime.

While volunteering, people get to know you and your abilities when you're not nervous. That's a lot better way to meet someone who could be your next boss or coworker than in an interview situation. In fact, if you've got a particular company in mind, you may even find out if that company supports volunteers through a particular charity in the area. Volunteer to work for that charity and you've got a good chance to meet someone who's working for the company at which you'd like to work.

Don't just start talking about your job search as soon as you meet them. Work with them on a project and then subtly work into the conversation that you're out of work. Give them an opportunity to offer to help you. If they don't take the hint, you may need to try to ask directly, but give the person the chance to make the offer because people always work harder for you if they are the ones that offer to help.

You may find that you just can't get into the right frame of mind on your own and you're not the type of person who volunteers. You may need to seek professional help. If you can't afford to pay for a career counselor, find out what types of career services might be offered by your state career center. The state may even have counselors available at little or no cost. You may find that your best bet is to consider a training program to have a better chance of getting the job you want. Whatever you decide to do to get yourself in the right frame of mind, just be sure it gets you out of the house and gives you the opportunity to work on improving your mood.

When you feel ready, it's time to work on your resume and begin your job search. I start exploring that process in the next chapter.

RECAP: You may need longer than one week to complete the tasks in this chapter. Don't be discouraged if you need to take longer than a week, but before you move on to Chapter 5, be sure you:

- Re-evaluate your career and make sure you are doing what you want to do. Reassess your skills and the type of jobs that you are prepared to do.
- Know how you like to work.
- Seek professional help if you're having trouble deciding what to do next.
- If needed, take tests to find out more about yourself, your skills and what you'd like to do.

CHAPTER 5

Weeks 4–8: The Job Search

YOU'RE READY TO start your job search. Now you've got to put together a game plan for that search. During these weeks, we'll focus on crafting various iterations of your resume, evaluating your job prospects, building your job search network, and contacting employers and employment agencies.

Your Job-Search Workspace

Before we get down to business, let's briefly discuss your job search work environment. Setting up daily at your kitchen table may be your only option, but if possible, try to establish a permanent workspace. Hopefully you have a small home office where your computer and printer are located. If you normally share this with your spouse, children, or housemates, you may need to negotiate squatting rights and set up the office in a way that best suits your work habits. This is one of the sacrifices those around you will need to make so you can work efficiently. If you're constantly looking for supplies or having to layout your workspace, then put away what you've been working on to make room for someone else, then lay out your workspace again the next day, it can get cumbersome and give you an easy excuse to not "set up" that day.

It goes without saying, but your job search will be a lot easier if you have a quiet place to work each day. If you're really stuck for finding that place, your church, synagogue, or organization for which you volunteer may have a spare room you can use. You can also visit your local library in which there are computers, wireless Internet, and quiet rooms that you can often reserve in advance for an uninterrupted work period. As a very last resort, many coffee shops and cafés have free wi-fi and can serve as a place to work until you find something more permanent.

Next, you'll need to set up a work schedule. Getting back into a daily routine is critical for your search to be effective, as well as for your sanity. Most people find they can work on the job search for about four hours a day. That includes making phone calls and appointments, getting job leads, and researching job opportunities online or elsewhere. Block off about four hours that you will spend in the office each day. At first, you may find it difficult to work for those four hours, but stay in the office even if you only end up surfing the web—the routine will help you establish good job-search habits. Occasionally, you'll want to change it up and get out of the office for a networking meeting. You'll need to determine what works best for you.

Once you start interviewing, that routine will be disrupted, but that's a good thing! As you cut into your office time, make sure you're still achieving your job prospecting goals, which should pay off in more interviews. As you make progress, the time you spend on your job search may expand to up to eight hours as you'll also need to send thank you notes to the people with whom you network and interview.

Your Resume

If you haven't written a resume or job searched for ten years or more, you'll need to totally change your idea of how to get out a resume. Today's web-enabled world of iPhones, BlackBerries, and other PDAs gives you many more ways to conduct a job search, as well as send a resume.

Forget snail mail. You may post your resume to a corporate website or e-mail it. Don't expect to print 100 copies for mailing. You'll only need a few copies to bring to interviews, but other than that you'll send your resumes via e-mail. (Since you may bring a slightly different resume to each interview, only print them out just before the interview.)

Companies can receive more than 1,000 resumes for each job posted, so a real person may never even see your resume—screenings are often done by computer. The software program scans for keywords specific to the job opening. If your resume doesn't include the requisite keywords, you will have little chance of your resume being seen by anybody responsible for hiring.

Even if an HR rep does sort through the resumes, the initial screening will be done in a matter of seconds per resume. As such, you've got to hit the key points in the opening paragraph or two or on your cover letter; the opening paragraph shouldn't be a listing of your job-search goals, but instead a showcase of your accomplishments. Before delving into the specifics about resume writing, here are the key elements.

Resume Rules—Then and Now

The landscape for developing resumes has changed dramatically over the past ten years. Before you start to write your resume, put these antiquated job-search ideas out of your mind and focus on what's being done today.

Old Rule: Limit Your Resume to One Page

This is no longer true. Be sure to give yourself enough space to highlight your critical skills and experience. But don't write a book. Keep your resume to two pages, unless you're in academia (these resumes can be longer if experience warrants it).

Old Rule: References Available Upon Request

It used to be common for people to put the phrase "References available upon request." You don't need it anymore. Everyone assumes that to be the case.

Old Rule: Show Every Job You Ever Held

If you've been working for ten years or longer, you don't have to list all of the jobs you have had. Not only will that date you, but it will also give you little room to play up accomplishments in the jobs that are most appropriate for the position you seek.

Remember, whether it's a computer program scanning your resume or a real person spending just seconds looking at it, you don't want it to include extraneous information. You want your resume to be packed with keywords that say, "Yes, I'm the perfect person for the position you need to fill." As you read the job requirements, note keywords that you can work into your resume.

Remember, your resume should be a marketing piece that highlights the most appropriate aspects of your career for the job you'd like to land. Don't include every detail of your working life—you're not writing a history book, you're promoting yourself. Think of this as your resume's only purpose: to get you in the door for an interview. You're the only one who can sell yourself. That's why it doesn't make sense to print 100 resumes. You may need to tweak every resume you send to match the keywords specific to each job as you apply for it.

Old Rule: Show Only a Ten-Year Job History

Don't limit your job history to the past ten years. Only highlight jobs that best match the position for which you are applying. List the positions that are most relevant to that which you are seeking, no matter how long ago you worked in that position.

Old Rule: One Resume Fits All

You don't need to craft one resume that you use for every position. In today's world, you're probably better off creating several resumes if you are seeking different types of positions. Each resume can highlight your past work experience that best matches the type of work you seek.

Your resume need not be limited to paid work, either. You may have volunteered for many years, while you earned money doing something else. If you want to pursue your next job based on the skills you learned as a volunteer, craft a resume based on your successes in that role. If the question comes up during an interview you can explain it was volunteer work.

Old Rule: Print Your Resume on Quality Stationery

In the past, you probably printed your resume on top quality linen stationery. These days, it doesn't pay off, so don't bother spending the money on this. In most cases you'll be sending your resume via e-mail in response to an online job posting. Sending a snail mail resume will date you! Or worse, your resume could arrive after the initial selection of interviewees has been made.

If you get into the habit of printing out copies of your resume only as you need them, you can tailor each resume specifically to the job for which you are applying by adding the appropriate keywords.

Resume Mechanics

Even if you've sent your resume by e-mail or posted it using an online job site, you should always bring a copy with you to an interview. Many times your resume prints out differently than intended when you send it electronically, so bring a properly formatted, clean copy with you.

Most people create their resume using Microsoft Word, which creates a ".doc" extension. It's wise to also prepare a resume in "text" format (".txt") that you can cut and paste into online forms. The reason for this: If you cut and paste from a Word doc, you'll also copy formatting codes that are not compatible with the online form, and you'll have to correct a bunch of strange errors.

SAVING A TEXT DOCUMENT

Click on file and hit "Save As." In the field "Save as Type," click on the down arrow. Select "Plain Text." You should also give the document a different name. For example, if you named your resume "Financial Advisor" you might want to call this one "Financial Advisor Plain Text," so you can quickly differentiate the document when you search your list of documents.

You will get a warning that you'll lose all formatting, pictures, and objects in the file. That's okay. You want to lose those things in a plain text document. You'll be given the option to save it using Windows (which will be the default), MS DOS, or other encoding. Use the Windows default.

After you've save the document, open it in the new plain text version. Fix any problems created when you lost the formatting. It might be a lot of work, but it's much easier to do it on your PC than do it each time you cut and paste your resume into an online form.

Meet Your Future Employer's Needs

Before you set out to write your resume, research jobs by reading postings on key online job search engines (such as *www.careerbuilder.com* and *www.monster.com*, more on this later in the chapter). Read the detailed job descriptions carefully and pick out the keywords commonly used by employers. For each type of job you are seeking, you will probably find up to ten to twenty keywords. Keep these in mind as you develop your resume. Be sure you include the same keywords throughout your resume.

For example, suppose you decided you'd like to work as a customer service representative. Reviewing several postings on Careerbuilder.com, I found these skills listed:

- Proven customer service skills
- Excellent telephone skills
- Effective written communication skills
- Ability to work with difficult people
- Ability to complete a customer service training program
- Basic computer skills

When applying for a customer service position, you would use this type of list to develop your resume. Make sure the job descriptions on your resume demonstrate successes in as many of the skill areas listed in the posting as possible. Also make sure you use the same words in your resume as those found in the advertisement.

Your online research should give you all you need to develop a list of keywords. You should feel free to repeat keywords in several descriptions of your past jobs if appropriate.

Remember, the computer software only searches for keywords. Even if a person is scanning the resumes, he or she is not likely the one making hiring decisions. In a big company, all screening is done by HR first, usually by a lower-level employee who is working from a list provided by the hiring manager. The employee wants to please the hiring manager by finding resumes that best match the list. Make it easy for them to pick yours.

Hiring managers often tell their HR staff that they just want to see the top ten or twenty resumes. You can only be one of those top ten or twenty resumes if your resume is as close to a perfect match as possible. That means you need to show your knowledge and experience meets their wish list. That's why I can't stress enough the importance of tweaking every resume you send for the specific position description you find.

Focus with Keywords

As you write your resume, hone in on the skills that meet the needs of each employer's job description. Select jobs you worked in over the years that best match the job for which you plan to apply. This could mean highlighting a job you did five to ten years ago.

For example, if you're building your resume for a customer service position, you should start that resume with a "Career Highlights" section at the top of the resume that clearly shows your experiences directly related to the key skills for the position.

After you finish writing the highlights section, jot down a brief description for each position that includes some of the keywords and skills sets. For example, if you worked in retail sales and had to calm difficult customers, highlight that job and the customer service skills you mastered in that position. Or if you ran events for a volunteer organization and were responsible for the crowd control, you can highlight that position.

Remember, you don't have to shy away from using the same keywords in several jobs descriptions. Computer scanning programs score the resume and you get the highest score by having more years doing each of the required skills. If a person is quickly scanning through the resume, this makes it easier for him to find the keywords and you can increase your chances of moving into the interview pile.

Showcase your Accomplishments

When writing your job descriptions, focus on your key accomplishments in each job. Use active verbs such as "developed," "established," "implemented," "led," or "organized" to show your successes.

Also try to quantify your successes when possible or appropriate. For example, suppose while you were working in a retail store you were responsible for selling $1 million worth of merchandise in a year, state that. Putting a number to your successes helps to show your future employer what you can do. But do be truthful. If a company checks out your claims and finds them to be false, you'll lose the opportunity.

Even if you quantify something not related to the specific position, company recruiters look for a signs you succeeded in the past. Putting together your successes on paper gives them the evidence they need. You show them that you did produce in former jobs and will produce for their company.

Update your Resume Language

You may be tempted to take an old resume and just reuse old job descriptions. Before using those descriptions, be certain you aren't using outdated terminology. As I'm sure you know, each market has its own type of "industry speak." You can show yourself, and your skills, to be outdated if you can't talk the talk. You do yourself a disservice if you ignore current industry jargon.

Carefully scour old job descriptions that you think you might want to reuse. Be sure to first read through industry publications from professional associations. As you find information on industry websites, if you aren't already familiar with them, note the catchphrases and other terms that are commonly used today. You may find that these are different from terms you've been using with your friends during the last decade. If this is the case, make sure to update your job descriptions with more recent terms and phrases.

As you review job postings in your industry, see what types of technologies are needed for the jobs that are available. Your former employer may have had antiquated systems, but you should assume you'll be expected to at least have a working knowledge of your industry's latest hardware and software. Proficiency is preferred. If your skills are rusty, you'll want to update them before applying for work. Adult-education classes at a local community college are a good place to start, and online courses are also plentiful. If you have trouble locating a course, contact the company that makes the hardware or software, as they often offer online or training centers in different regions of the country.

When you've finished the course, you may not be ready to jump into work using that software, but at least you'll understand the key terms and functions, so you can make a better impression on the interview. Showing that you've taken a course lets you add the keywords you need to your resume.

Writing Your Resume

Now that you know your keywords and have developed brief descriptions for each of the positions in your job history that you want to highlight, writing the actual resume will be easier. As you write your resume keep these points in mind:

Keep It Short and Simple

While you don't have to limit your resume to just one page, don't let it expand to more than two pages. That could hurt you. There's little-to-no chance that the person scanning resumes will read the entire document. In fact, some may even be turned off if it's too wordy. Remember the KEYwords are the key. You only need to highlight the positions that align with the company's keywords for the position in question. You don't need to tell your life story. You just want to get your foot in the door.

Keep It Professional, Not Personal

Don't include information about your family or hobbies, unless the information is relevant to the job. You also shouldn't include your height, age, weight, sex, or religion, unless it's somehow related to the position. For example, if you are applying to work at your church or synagogue, you certainly want to indicate your religious affiliation.

Stay on Point

Be sure every bit of information on your resume relates to the position you want to land. You should not include non-work experience unless it helps you to demonstrate skills that are relevant to the job. Suppose, for example, you enjoy wood-working and you're seeking a position in which those types of skills are needed. In that case, it would be helpful to include information about your hobby. Otherwise leave it off!

Address Work Gaps

You've been laid off, so you will have a work gap. You should briefly address that time and spin it in a positive way. For example, suppose you've been volunteering for a community group and you organized a major event. During that time, you may have learned skills that could be useful in this next position. Or, you may have gone back to school to learn a new trade or new skills, which also looks good to potential employers.

Formatting Your Resume

There are many ways to organize and craft your resume, and many good books available that focus solely on the resume (see Resources). The format presented here gives a solid example of what's commonly seen today in the marketplace.

In the past, resumes were formatted in chronological order. That may not be the best thing for you if you've been in the work force ten to twenty years. Also, if you decide you want to change fields, it's possible that your hobbies or volunteer work may be more relevant than your most recent jobs.

For those of you looking to change careers or those of you older than forty, you may want to construct a resume that highlights your functional skills rather than one written in chronological order. I don't think I need to show you how to format a chronological resume, you've probably done that once before, but here are the parts of a functional resume, which you might want to consider as an option:

Basic Information: Include name, address, telephone number (be sure to list the number where you are most easily reached), and e-mail address. Do not neglect to include your e-mail address, as many HR departments prefer to contact candidates initially via e-mail rather then play phone tag.

Highlights or Summary: Summarize the highlights of your career. Be sure to use the keywords that match the list you compiled researching the necessary job skills for the type of position you are seeking.

Experience: Instead of listing your work history, prepare a series of paragraphs that talk about your skills. Using keywords you've found, show that you have the skills they seek in an employee. For example, looking at the skill list for the customer service position previously discussed, you would write a paragraph about proven customer service skills, excellent telephone skills, effective written communication skills, ability to work with difficult people, ability to complete a customer service training program, and basic computer skills. Write these paragraphs using brief sentences that highlight your accomplishments.

Work History: Use this section to provide a list of your previous jobs in chronological order. Each job can be just one line that includes your job title, your company, and your dates of employment.

Education: List your degrees and the schools you attended. If you took courses that match keywords you need, highlight it here.

Certifications or Technical Skills: If you have related certifications or technical skills that are relevant to the type of job you seek, include them in this section.

Turn the page to see what this resume would look like.

Name
Address
City, State, Zip
Telephone Number(s)
E-mail Address

Summary or Highlights *use either of these terms*

Write no more than two or three sentences that summarize or highlight previous accomplishments that relate directly to the position you are seeking. *Think: keywords.*

Experience

Skill One: *i.e. Customer Service Skills*
Write a brief summary that highlights your successes in this area.
Skill Two: *i.e. Telephone Skills*
Write a brief summary that highlights your successes in this area.
Skill Three:
and so on until you highlight each of the skills you've determine are important for the position you are seeking

Work History

Job Title   Employer   Years Worked
List your jobs in chronological order. You don't have to go back more than ten years, but do show older experience if the jobs are relevant to what you want to do next.

Education

Degree, School Attended, Year Completed
Course Emphasis *if appropriate*

Certifications

If you have any related certifications or technical skills include them in this section

Proof Carefully

You could be the perfect person for the job, but if the hiring manager sees typos on your resume, don't expect an interview. Errors on the resume indicate that you are not detail-oriented. Your resume likely will end up in the circular file.

Even if you think you're a great proofreader or are relying on your word processing system's spellchecker (this is not recommended, by the way), ask at least three other people to proof your resume carefully. No one is a perfect proofreader. When I worked at *Popular Photography* magazine, we had at least five people read every article, at least one of whom was a copy editor that specialized in proofreading and we still found typos in each issue! Everyone's eyes tend to see what they expect to see when they proof something.

One trick that helps is to read every sentence backwards. When you read the sentence in the opposite direction you look more carefully at each word. Using this method you won't necessarily catch grammatical errors or errors involving word usage, but it should help you catch misspellings.

Networking 101

While the web is a very valuable tool to help you search for descriptions of positions, don't expect to land a job solely by answering those postings. If the posting appears on a site such as monster.com, your resume will be one of roughly 500 that are submitted. The odds just aren't in your favor.

Too many people spend most of their time searching for and applying for jobs they find posted online or listed in the newspaper. These are not the people who land the jobs. Studies show that 80 percent of jobs are filled through networking and only 20 percent are filled from applying to postings. As such, it stands to reason that you should spend 80 percent of your time networking to find a job and dedicate 20 percent of your time to applying to online ads. While it can't hurt to apply, don't count on getting a response.

Your network will do more to help you find a job. Spending hour after hour in front of your computer writing the best resume in the world along with top-notch cover letters won't be worth much if you don't first build and nurture your network.

Here are six steps to follow when embarking on a networking plan:

1. *What Are Your Goals?*—Write down your goals. Think about what you hope to gain by networking. Are you looking for self-improvement ideas, do you want to learn about potential jobs, explore developments in your field, discover training opportunities, seek emotional support? The truth is, you probably want to do all of this. And think about what you have to offer in return. Networking is about sharing.

2. *Contacts Are Key*—Next, write down the types of people with whom you'd like to network, including their background, leisure traits, personality traits, job position, and values. Then make a list of people to add to your networking list. Next make a list of people you'd like to have in your network, but don't know yet. Decide how you will approach these potential contacts—by phone, e-mail, chat rooms, online discussion groups, or in-person meetings. You probably will use a mix of these options.

3. *Get "Linked In"*—The Internet has something for everyone, and yes, there's a site that helps you get and stay networked with others in your industry. Linked In (*www.linkedin.com*) is a giant electronic directory allowing you to post information about yourself, read it about others, and contact them. It's a place to seek

employment as well. At the time of writing, it had 24 million members in 150 industries.

4. *Information Interviews*—For the people you don't know yet, but with whom you'd like to network, consider lining up information interviews. These are a great way to find out about what it's really like to work in an industry with which you might be unfamiliar, and about jobs you didn't know existed or those that might be funded in the near future. Before setting up any interviews, learn all you can about the type of work you are considering, so you can make a good impression and ask insightful questions. People you do know can help connect you to the contacts you want to make, but if you don't know the person, it's okay to contact them using a brief personal note. Their time is extremely valuable so make sure you are specific about what you want to learn when requesting an appointment. Give them the option of setting it up online or follow up by phone. Make it clear that you're not seeking a specific job, but want to learn more about the job opportunities in their industry. Treat the informational interview as you would a "real" interview. Dress the part, be on time, and bring the most recent copy of your resume in the off chance that the contact requests one. For the most part, people enjoy talking about themselves and what they do, so there's no need to be overly nervous. Be sure to ask open-ended questions and listen carefully. Don't overstay your welcome. Be sure to ask up front how much time they have and stick to their time limit unless they invite you to stay longer. As you finish the interview, ask for recommendations of others you can talk with for more information. Follow up promptly with a thank-you note in which you mention a key piece of information or

personal fact you learned from the interview so your new contact does not feel as if he wasted his time.

5. *Take Action*—You'll need to organize your list of contacts in a way that makes sense to you—either in a contacts database or hard copy—before establishing a plan for reaching out to those contacts. You may decide you want to make one cold call or e-mail (contact with someone you don't know, possibly to set up an information interview), meet someone for lunch, and reconnect with two others in your network each day. Make notes in the individual records for each person you contact, including the key information you discussed during the contact, so you'll have the information for follow-up contact later.

6. *Keep Building*—Your network is something that will never be complete. You should always be looking to expand your network and expand your horizons, even when you are not looking for a job. No one will help you in the future if the only time they hear from you is when you need something from them.

   Stay in touch even when you don't need something. Call them. Meet them for lunch. Arrange for a social gathering with a number of people in your network who all enjoy doing the same things. Look for opportunities to help people in your network. All those favors you do will pay off when you need something.

   Once you've got an active network in place, you won't have any trouble tapping into it for job leads and job introductions.

Remember, a slew of people answer each job posting, whether it's posted online or in a newspaper. If you want your resume to get to the desk of the person making the job hiring decision, it behooves you to have an inside contact. With so many people coming through HR, a known entity recommended by an associate or friend often is more likely to make it to the top of a job interview list.

Support Groups and Online Networks

Another way to network is to join groups. You will want to do some research and find out which groups meet in person and which groups exist solely in the virtual space. The most common type of group for job seekers are support groups. These are run primarily by civic and religious organizations. Another good place to seek support is your industry's professional or trade association. You may also find support groups made up of alumni of your former company.

Job Search Support Groups

When considering job search support groups, first do your research. Contact the organizer to find out about the group's structure; you'll want to know how gatherings are conducted and who moderates them. Research who's behind the meetings and the level of professional support the group has for its operations. If there isn't a counselor, human resources professional, or clergyman involved, the meetings may be more akin to bitch sessions than a positive environment in which you can further your job search.

You'll find some job groups are organized around regular speakers for motivation or learning job-search skills, while others emphasize sharing job leads and networking. Some meetings and forums are structured more like a lecture, while others tend to be structured around sharing emotions as well as sharing job tips and leads.

Both types of groups can help. How you feel when you leave the group will help dictate whether it is worth your time. If you find your mood is lifted, continue going. If you leave the space feeling depressed or more anxious, you should join another group.

Before entering a group setting, know what you want to get from the experience. Is it job-searching tips? Job leads? Or do you merely need someone to talk to after working alone at home all day? The most important thing you'll get from a well-run support group is a place to go where people can relate to your situation. Group members help support you through the process.

Support groups shouldn't become your main priority for easing the pain of losing your job. They have a valid place in your job search as long as you don't become a support group junky, always looking for your next fix!

Professional or Trade Associations

These groups are a goldmine for networking and job leads. If you're not a member of your professional or trade association, contact them immediately and see what it costs to join. If you can afford to do so, don't hesitate to send the check. It's a worthy investment.

If you can't afford the membership fee, find out if the association makes provisions for nonmembers who were recently laid off. You may be able to attend meetings and access closed portions of the website with a temporary membership until you land your next job. Join the association as soon as possible after you find employment because it can provide a great source of information as you continue to build your career.

If the association doesn't allow for temporary memberships, consider volunteering with them. As a volunteer you'll work closely with those employed in your industry—people who can serve up job leads or introduce you to your next boss. If you demonstrate stellar performance as a volunteer, your talents should be recognized quickly, perhaps with rewards to follow!

Employee Alumni Groups

After a major layoff, it's not uncommon to find former employee groups crop up. You may find that these groups give you a great way to gather information about professional contacts working in your industry. Connecting with these groups also allows you to stay in touch with old friends socially to keep your spirits up.

However, if spending time in these forums feels more like time spent in a morgue, steer clear of them. If your alumni meetings leave you feeling depressed, stop going. During this time, it's important to connect with people who energize you and encourage you to push forward with your job search.

Tapping the Web

While answering online job postings to land work is a long shot, you'll still find a wealth of useful information on the web. You can research how to improve your job searching skills, as well as do research about the companies you plan to approach. The more you know about a company, the better you can target your cover letter and your resume to match the company's needs. When you do get that interview, you'll also present yourself as a much stronger candidate. So don't only think of the web as a communication and jobs-search tool. Plan to use it for research so you can make the best impression when you get in the door.

Job Search Websites

Most people looking for a job will visit such well-known websites as Career Builder (*www.careerbuilder.com*), Monster (*www.monster.com*), or Yahoo! Hot Jobs (*www.hotjobs.yahoo.com*). But there are many other options! The big websites may have lots of job listings, but they also get lots of visitors, so that means you'll be competing with perhaps thousands of applicants for each job.

If you belong to a professional association, their job boards are a great place to start. If not, check out Google's directory (*www .google.com/Top/Business/Employment/Job_Search*), which lists more than 300 job-search sites. You'll find job sites organized by industry, entry level and internships, job fairs, executive search, recruiters, seasonal, staffing services, and worldwide.

In addition to job posting sites, here you'll find sites with resume and interviewing advice.

To Post or Not to Post?

Before you post your resume online, carefully consider the pros and cons. Posting a resume online is akin to posting an ad about yourself that anyone can read, even people you may not want to hear from, such as spammers or scammers. Be aware that if you do decide to post your resume you could receive garbage e-mail. That said, you never know who might find you, so if you're willing to risk some spam it might be worthwhile.

The first step is to secure a secondary e-mail address for which you'll use solely as a contact for online postings (Yahoo or Google offer free web-based e-mail services). By having a place online specifically for e-mail generated from your online resume, when you've found a job you can just ignore it or better yet, take it down.

Using this kind of secondary e-mail address gives you an extra measure of protection against viruses, and also limits the amount of e-mail that comes into your main account. When you respond to a legitimate e-mail, give the recruiter your primary e-mail address and let him contact you there in the future.

If you post your resume online and it's more than one page, add keywords to the bottom of your second page to capture the attention of recruiters. Here's a sneaky way to work them in: Change the text color for the keywords to white before posting your resume. By changing the color, the keywords won't show if a recruiter prints your resume, but the scanning software will still pick them up!

Company Websites

Company websites are a great place to find job postings that get fewer hits than those at big online job search sites. You can find a wealth of information about position descriptions (think: keywords), but you also can discover a great deal about the company, its mission and goals, and its future plans.

Take the time to read the most recent annual report. This will help you understand the company's history and its specific map of the coming year. You may have perused annual reports before, focusing on easy-to-read marketing copy with stylized photos, but you glossed over fine print, where you'll find the most useful information. The Management's Discussion and Analysis and the Notes to the Financial Statements will give you specifics about a company's future plans. Once you have a good idea of where the company wants to go, you can use that information to develop your cover letter using keywords that match the company's growth plans.

If you read about something in the works that would be a perfect fit for you, use the company's verbiage as you develop your cover letter and spell out any prior experience that directly relates to the upcoming project. You could hit just the right chord and be picked out of the pack of hundreds of applicants just because you showed that you did your homework, making you a good potential asset for the company.

Other Job-Hunting Techniques

In addition to your targeted online search and your networking efforts, which should undoubtedly be where your focus lies, here are a few more techniques that can be added to the mix.

Perusing the Ads

While I don't suggest that you make this your primary method of finding jobs, you will get ideas about which companies are hiring. Let's take a quick look at more traditional ways people use to find out which companies are hiring:

Newspapers—Most daily and weekly newspapers have an employment section. Usually the best day to use the daily newspaper's employment section is Sunday. Most post the job listings to their website, which is a lot faster than looking through pages and pages of job ads that don't interest you.

Grocery Stores—You may not think a grocery store is a likely place to job search, but many of the larger chains have boards where people post . . . jobs . . . items for sale . . . pets, etc. Often a small business that doesn't want to be inundated with resumes and that wants to hire a local will post here. If you find yourself in need of quick cash to help get you by, you might be able to find an odd job on these boards.

Community Centers, Churches, and Synagogues—If you belong to a community center, a church or synagogue, you may find that other members post available jobs on a bulletin board. If not, they may call the leader of your church or synagogue with job leads. Don't hesitate to make a contact with your community center, church or synagogue to see what type of job resources they offer.

Cold Calling Employers

After you've done all your online research, you may decide that there are a few companies you'd like to target. You can respond to jobs via e-mail, but you also may want to cold call potential employers.

If you do decide to cold call, try to make it more of a warm call. Find the names of key people who are working in the companies that interest you. Send them an e-mail message and try to set up an informational interview. Make it clear that you just want to find out more about the industry. Don't ask for a job on that informational interview, but do ask if they can recommend someone who you can talk with about possible openings.

There are many websites you can use to help turn cold calls into warm calls. Some of my favorites include:

- Hoovers (*www.hoovers.com*), which specializes in information on companies, industries, and people in those industries.
- Vault (*www.vault.com*), where you can find information about companies, industries, and salaries. You'll also find rankings by industry.
- Wetfeet (*www.wetfeet.com*), where you'll find lots of great career information. My favorite spot on this website are

the insider guides that give you extensive details about career types.

The 411 on Employment Agencies

Employment agencies have a role, but don't make the mistake of thinking they are working for you unless you're paying their fee (and those fees can be as high as three to six months of your starting salary!). Many employment agencies won't spend time working to place you in a job unless you're making at least $100,000 a year. This is because when you earn less than that, the agencies can't earn enough on commissions to keep their business afloat.

Instead, you'll find most employment agencies work at the behest of the employer and serve as screeners for them. Their role is to reduce the numbers of candidates sent to an employer. Therefore, unless you're a perfect match, you won't get near the company.

It won't hurt you to contact as many agencies as you want, but don't expect to find a job that way. It's more a matter of luck and timing that you happen to contact an agency and happen to be an exact match for what the hiring company is looking for at the time.

Employment agencies will save your data and will call you if they get a perfect match, but don't hold your breath and whatever you do, don't sign an exclusive agreement with a search firm. It will just limit your exposure and opportunities.

Job Fairs

Because at most booths, you'll only get seconds to speak with company representatives, this is one of the least effective means of searching for a job. The most you can expect to gain from these events is submission of your resume into several company databases.

You may be able to improve your chances of getting a follow up call if you go the websites of the companies that will be at the show, review the positions that are available in advance, and create a keyword-heavy resume for each.

A Job Search Is a Marathon, Not a Sprint

Remember: Your job search is more akin to a marathon than a sprint. You need to stay focused and stay on-task for the long haul. If you do a lot of sprints and then get tired and give up for a while in between each sprint, it will take you longer to land a job.

The job searcher who consistently works for a set number of hours each day following an established routine has a much better chance of building up the needed network to find her next position.

RECAP: You may need longer than one week to complete the tasks in this chapter. Don't be discouraged if you need to take longer than a week, but before you move on to Chapter 6, be sure you:

- Set up a quiet place where you can work each day and determine a daily work routine.
- Update your resume focusing on what you really want to do.
- Be ready to send your resume electronically, as well as by hard copy.
- Be sure to fill your resume with keywords for the jobs you want.
- Build and nurture a network of people who can help you find your next job.

- Join supports groups that help you build your confidence and your job search energy. Avoid support groups that make you feel depressed.
- Do lots of online research, focusing on companies in the industry so you're well-prepared for your interviews.

CHAPTER 6

Week 9: The Job Interview

AFTER ALL THE hard work of finding job leads, you've finally hooked a fish and it's time to reel him in—you've got an interview! You want to make your mark because getting in the door is the hard part. In this chapter, expect lots of tips to help you feel polished for your interview.

Interview Preparation

The key to getting through this difficult—but exciting—period of time is to make sure you have done all your homework and you come across as confident and calm. They often say luck is simply being prepared when opportunity presents itself. In order to make a little luck for yourself, here are some tried-and-true methods to get you ready for your big day.

Calming Techniques

You might expect tips about how to answer difficult questions, which you will find below, but first let's talk about mental prep for this difficult process. Almost everyone gets nervous before an interview. Some people deny it and have a very calm exterior, but there are few people who can conduct an interview in total calm unless they use mental exercises to help get them there.

While these tips won't transform you into a Zen master by the time of your interview, they should help calm you down enough to think and answer questions strategically. Too often, people find their nerves screw up their chances of performing well on an interview, even though they've done the homework, researched the company, and made sure they can clearly tell an interviewer how their skills match the job. Nerves may make you forget everything, including your name!

You must find a way to calm down. The more relaxed you are before and during an interview, the better you'll come across to the hiring manager. Quieting your mind allows you to focus on what needs to be conveyed—your personality and talent.

When you feel calm during an interview, you're in a better state of mind to communicate clearly. You're also more aware of negative impressions the interviewer may have and can try to correct them right away. We'll delve into that more in the coming sections.

There are different types of stress-reduction techniques. Some take a lot of practice, such as meditation, yoga, and T'ai Chi; others you can learn quickly and use successfully. We'll focus on some that are easy to learn, but if you're already familiar with meditation, yoga, or T'ai Chi, use whatever you know works for you.

Visualization

First, pick something that makes you feel relaxed, such as a walk along the beach or watching a sunset. Close your eyes and picture yourself at your favorite serene spot. Focus on this image for two or three minutes. When you are able to concentrate on the picture and remove any other thoughts, you'll be amazed at how quickly this can settle you down.

If you need some help, a CD of nature sounds can help get you there. Listen to it while you visualize going to your calming place. On the day of your interview bring a photo that depicts your favorite place and play the CD in your car as you drive there. That will help you use visualization to calm down.

You may even want to paste the image to the inside of the notebook you bring to the interview. Use the visualization technique while you are waiting to be greeted by your interviewer. It should help you maintain a sense of composure, especially if your nerves flare up while waiting. For those who tend to worry a lot before an interview this relaxation technique works well. Looking at a relaxing image takes the place of worrying.

Deep Breathing

Deep breathing is a great way to release tension in your entire body. Take a long deep breath through your nose for four or five seconds, then hold your breath for another four to five seconds, and finally breathe out through your mouth for four to five seconds. You'll know it's working if you feel a sense of relaxation come over you, especially in your chest, shoulders and any tense muscles.

Repeat this method of deep breathing for at least two to three minutes. The first few times you try this you may need to make some noise as you breathe in deeply to help get you started. After you've practiced doing this for a while, you'll find you don't need to make the noise and will still benefit from deep breathing quietly.

You certainly don't want to do this noisily while waiting to be interviewed. You'll attract too much attention and may make a negative impression. Most will think you're really nervous if they hear you deep breathing. Or worse, some may think it's the sign of a medical emergency! You certainly don't want to bring unnecessary attention to yourself while you wait. But this relaxation technique can help you feel less tense and allows you to sit in a more relaxed position which will allow you to present yourself as calm and confident in the interview.

Thought Blocking

If you're someone who constantly worries that you may say something wrong or have already done so, you may want to try thought blocking. Others who benefit from thought blocking are people who tend to frequently criticize themselves as they think through the answers to questions rather than really listening to what the interviewer is asking. Instead of being critical of your performance, you should instead be focusing on what you want to say next.

Thought blocking helps you control unwanted thoughts. If you are constantly thinking, "oh no, I shouldn't have said that," or some other critical phrase, practice stopping yourself in everyday conversation.

Each time you start feeling self-critical just say the word "stop" quietly to yourself. Don't say it out loud or people will start looking at you as if you are weird and wondering what you want them to stop doing. You may want to add the practice of deep breathing when you say "stop" to help you release tension and clear negative thoughts from your mind.

This relaxation technique should help you gain more control over what you are thinking and give you the opportunity to concentrate on what you need to say in the interview.

Develop an Interview Checklist

I'm a big believer in preparing lists, especially when I expect to be nervous about doing something. Everyone tends to forget things when they are nervous. You can calm those nerves if you have a list ready and can go down the list to be sure you're prepared.

So the day before an interview, use the checklist below to make sure you haven't forgotten anything and assure yourself that you're ready to make a great impression.

Job Interview Checklist

TASK	DONE
Be ready to discuss five things that make you the right candidate for the job.	❐
Be ready to discuss everything you have on your resume.	❐
Be prepared to discuss your education or technical training and why it qualifies you for this job.	❐
Know which hobbies you want to highlight, if any, that are relevant to this job.	❐
Know the details on your resume so that you can fill out a job application that matches that detail accurately. This becomes critical if you want to remember to use those keywords. Also make a list of the addresses and contact numbers for former employers and anyone you want to use as a reference.	❐
Be sure you have your Social Security number, driver's license, and proof of any certifications you'll need.	❐

Job Interview Checklist

TASK	DONE
Be sure you have the directions you need to get to the interview and you know the driving time. If you are traveling somewhere for the first time and it's within a reasonable distance to your home, drive the route and time it before the day of your interview.	☐
Have a list of questions you plan to ask about the company.	☐

I recommend you review the checklist the day before the interview, so you have time to fix any last-minute problems. You should also take one more quick look at the checklist before you walk out the door on the day of the interview, just to be sure you're not forgetting anything—like your Social Security card, driver's license, or other documentation you planned to bring with you.

The night before the interview be certain you get a good night's sleep, even if it means taking a mild sleeping pill (such as Unisom or Tylenol Nighttime). But don't take something you've never taken before. You don't want to wake up too groggy to do the interview, so you need to be sure you know how your body responds to the medication.

Morning of the Interview

When you wake up, use the relaxation technique that you practiced and you find works best. Don't let yourself get too worked up. Go through your checklist to be sure you have everything you need for the interview.

Get dressed in an outfit that is appropriate for the position to which you are applying. If you're smart you'll pick it out the day before so you don't have to worry about what to wear. For example, in picking the right outfit, you want to dress in a business suit (women may want to consider a business dress—not something you'd normally wear to go out in the evening) for an interview with a bank or most office jobs, but would likely dress in work clothes if you're applying at a construction work site. No matter where you are interviewing, your clothes should be cleaned and pressed. Even if you plan to go to an interview in a T-shirt, press it. You want to look your best. You don't want to look like you rolled out of bed and then ran to the interview.

Be sure to give yourself enough time to drive to the interview. If you haven't been to the interview location before, it's a good idea to drive to it prior to the interview. You certainly don't want to walk in the door late, nervous, and sweaty just because you got lost.

During the Interview

The interview starts as soon as you arrive. You may just be sitting in a waiting room for a while, but assistants to the person you will be interviewing could be keeping an eye on the applicants, so just assume your show starts as soon as you walk in the company's front door. Here are some tips to be sure you make a great first impression:

- If you got a ride with someone don't bring him inside to wait with you. Ask him to wait in the car or in a nearby coffee shop.
- Definitely don't chew gum, smoke a cigar or cigarette, or eat while you are waiting.
- Leave your sunglasses in the car. Dark sunglasses inside may make you look as though you are hiding something.
- Go to the ladies room if you want to apply makeup or comb your hair.

- Be nice to everyone you talk with, even the receptionist. You'll be surprised how many times a receptionist will give the interviewer comments about the type of first impression you make. If the decision is between you and one other person and the other person was better liked by others in the office, you could lose the opportunity.
- Don't use your cell phone within earshot of anyone in the office. If you want to make a call, wait until you get out of the building unless your interviewer asks for information about your former company or a reference and you don't have it handy. Then you may want to ask permission to call for the information. If you do end up calling, keep your conversation brief and to the point. You can call the person back after you get out of the office and explain the situation.
- While you're sitting and waiting, read company literature that's in the waiting room or read through your research notes. Don't just sit there and twiddle your thumbs looking nervous.
- Don't make a scene or look annoyed if the interviewer is running late. It's likely it's because he's interviewing someone else or in a meeting that ran long.

When you get inside the office, your first impression is critical. Your interviewer will quickly size you up by the way you are dressed and the way you shake hands. Usually it's best to let the interviewer extend his or her hand first. Your handshake should be firm, but not too hard. You'll want to adjust the firmness based on whether you are shaking the hand of a man or a woman. I've had men shake my hand so hard that it hurts.

As you start talking, stay aware of the interviewer's body language. This will help you determine whether or not the interviewer is comfortable talking with you. If you find the interviewer is very nervous and seems to be looking for a way to get you quickly out the door, you can try to make him more comfortable or just accept that it's not the right company for you and move on.

There are some things you might be able to do using body language to make both you and the interviewer more comfortable:

- Sit up straight and lean slightly forward in your chair. This will project the body language that you are interested and engaged in the conversation. As you talk stay aware of your interviewer's body language and try to position yourself in a way that mirrors him or her.
- Periodically nod or make positive gestures to show that you are interested in what he or she is saying, but don't become a bobbing head. Practice this talking with friends. If they ask why your head is bobbing so much, you're overdoing it.
- Don't try to sit too close to the interviewer. If you've pulled a chair near him or her be sure it's not invading his or her personal space. If you make the interviewer feel uncomfortable, you will shift the focus to that discomfort and away from your interview.
- Don't wear a perfume or cologne with a strong odor. Your interviewer could be allergic and that could end the interview more abruptly than expected.
- If your interview is interrupted, which does happen occasionally, don't stare at your interviewer or the person interrupting you. Instead offer to step out if they need privacy.
- If you're going to do the interview by phone, set up the phone near a mirror so you can watch your expressions. That will help you keep a smile on your face and your mood more positive. You also may find that standing during a phone interview helps to keep you more alert and allows you to be more involved in the conversation.

You also need to be aware of things you can do that may give your interviewer the idea that you're not interested in the job, so watch your body language carefully. Here are some things you definitely don't want to do:

- Rub the back of your head or neck even if you have a cramp. This gesture shows a lack of interest.
- Rub or touch your nose. This suggests dishonestly and can look gross.
- Fold your arms across your chest. This will make you look unfriendly and not engaged in the conversation.
- Cross your legs and shake one of them over the other. This will be distracting to your interviewer and gives the impression that you are nervous or uncomfortable.
- Lean your body toward the door. You may make your interviewer think you're ready to leave as soon as possible.
- Slouch back in your seat. You will look as though you're not prepared or not interested.
- Stare back blankly. This will look like you're distancing yourself from the conversation.

Explaining your Unemployment

You will need to talk about your unemployment. As we discussed in Chapter 2, know your story and be prepared to tell it. Don't talk negatively about your former employers or coworkers. You'll look like a complainer and will likely turn off the interviewer. Instead, if asked about something you didn't like about your former job, turn a negative into a positive by giving an example of how you corrected a problem and improved the working environment for everyone.

Don't Be Critical

You may have done a lot of research and have some good ideas for improvements, but you should never criticize the company for how it's doing things. Don't tell the interviewer that the company is doing something wrong and you know how to do it better. You don't want to appear combative or overly critical, but you should feel free to make gentle suggestions about how you could improve what they are doing.

Instead of risking being critical, you should use your research to develop a good set of questions that demonstrate you understand the company and its operations. This will help you show your interest. You'll also show how well prepared you are and that you did your homework.

Always show enthusiasm for the job even if it's something that you're planning to do just to make a few extra bucks until you find the right job. No one wants to hire someone who isn't even enthusiastic during the interview. If you're not excited about the job during the interview, your interviewer will certainly assume you're not going to be enthusiastic when you start work.

Dealing with Basic Questions

You should expect to be asked some basic questions that are asked on almost every interview, so take the time to prepare your answers at home and be ready to give your best answer that emphasizes the key points you want to make. The three most common interview questions are:

1. Tell me about yourself.
2. Why do you want to work here?
3. What are your goals?

These questions are actually ice breakers. How you answer them will set the tone for the entire interview, so think about your responses and how you want to answer them in the quiet of your home. You can influence the flow of the rest of the interview and have a better chance that the interviewer will focus on the key things you want to put forward.

But, remember these questions are ice breakers. The interviewer is not expecting a long-winded response. Keep your initial response brief and bring out the key points you want to make. If the interviewer is interested, he will then ask a follow up question about a specific point.

You can control where the interview goes, by saying just enough to pique the interviewer's interest and encouraging his desire to learn more. That way he asks more questions about what you want to talk about.

Tell Me About Yourself

You're not being asked to give your life history, so don't go into a story about your childhood and how you got to where you are. No one wants to hear your life story in a situation where they are meeting you for the first time. Instead, think about how you can answer this question briefly and get the interviewer engaged in you as a person—not just an interviewee. If you've done a good job of research, you should be able to pick a few experiences from your life that are relevant to the job you are seeking, point out a few job-related things and talk about any educational background that you have that is relevant.

Why Do You Want to Work Here?

With this question, the interviewer is testing your knowledge of the company and its products or its services. If you do your homework you should be well prepared to answer this question based on the research you did on the company's website.

Pick out a few things you want to talk about related to the company's goals and missions that you can tie directly to the type of position you are seeking. Don't be afraid to even use the company's wording as you develop your answer to this question.

What Are Your Goals?

With this question, the interviewer is testing how long you'll stay around on the job. He probably wants to know if you just want the job for a year or two or if you think it's something that will engage you for a lot longer.

Don't talk about goals you have outside the company unless they somehow relate to how you'll be staying around the area. For example, suppose you just bought a new home near the company.

If you are thinking of starting a small business or doing something else once you get settled in your new home and you know that this job is just a short-term bridge to get some extra bucks until you can start your business, definitely don't talk about that. Think about how you can answer this question to give the interviewer the impression that you will be at the job for a while. People hate going through the hiring process, so they will be less likely to hire you if they know from the start you are going to be a short-term employee.

For Industry Changers and People Over Forty

If you've been laid off, you're likely working for an industry that's facing a downturn and to find a job you may need to change industries. If you're older than forty your job search challenges will be even greater.

Many people who are laid off after the age of forty find that they have a very hard time getting past the tough questions that probably aren't asked of younger candidates. While age discrimination is against the law, there are lots of ways you can pick up clues that you may actually be sitting in front of someone who just doesn't want to hire you because you are an older worker.

The types of questions asked by an interviewer can certainly give you a clue to his or her age bias. In fact, if you are asked many of the questions in this section, it could be a sign that your age may be a barrier to your getting the job.

Tough questions for industry changers or older workers usually fall in one of two areas—questions related to your qualifications and questions related to your longevity with the company. If you are shifting careers or an older job seeker, be prepared to answer the following questions before you go in. Practice your answers, so you can respond calmly and in a way that will help you land the job.

AGE DISCRIMINATION AFTER FORTY

Don't be surprised if you recognize signs of age discrimination if you've been laid off after the age of forty and are looking for a new job. While it is illegal under the Age Discrimination in Employment Act (ADEA), you will find it's difficult to enforce and any enforcement will take longer than you can wait around for a job.

The ADEA states that there must be a lawful reason that is not connected to age when making employment decisions. You fall under the aegis of the ADEA if you are age forty and over and you are applying for, or working in, a company with at least twenty employees. The ADEA makes it unlawful for job ads or other materials to mention age requirements or state that a certain age is preferred, unless of course it falls under an exception. Note that sometimes age can be a factor in hiring. For example, if a director needs a teen to play a particular role in a play, he can decide not to hire a person over forty. A company also cannot set age limits for training it offers. Age can't be a factor in hiring decisions, when making decisions about promotion or when deciding whom to lay off.

If you are a victim of age discrimination, file a complaint with the Equal Employment Opportunity Commission (the company can't take action against you). But you'll be waiting months and possibly years for a settlement. At the same time, word likely will get out that you are a troublemaker, which can make it harder for you to find a job, especially if you are looking for one in a small, tightly knit industry. So if you do come across discrimination, deal with it to the best of your abilities and move on.

Qualification Questions

While all applicants are asked questions about their qualifications, the type of questions older workers are asked often differ. Here we'll look at some of the most difficult questions you could be asked and give you some ideas of how to answer them effectively. Handled properly, you may even be able turn a negative into a positive.

You're Overqualified. Won't You Get Bored?

I hate this question when I hear it. I'm sure you do (or will) too. You can deal with it effectively by talking about how impressed you are with the company and its products or services. Point out to your interviewer that your experience is exactly what the company needs and how your experience will allow you to hit the ground running. You won't need much training, which will save the company time and money.

This Company Is on the Fast Track. Can You Keep Up?

Imagine an employer asking someone in her twenties this question? It wouldn't happen, but you will hear it if you are older than forty. Sure, it's one of the clearest signs that age discrimination is lurking in the room, but don't get angry. Just realize that age discrimination is present and offset it by talking about your depth of knowledge that matches what the company needs and the strategies you use to stay current on all the issues related to your field, as well as how you keep up with technological changes. You can also discuss how you dealt with rapid change in your former company as well as how much you got done in a day on your last job. You may also want to add in a story about how you stay physically fit. You can show your interviewer that you are on the fast track by talking about your energy and attitudes.

Are Your Skills Transferable?

If you've recently been laid off, it most likely means that your industry is in a downturn and you'll have to look outside that industry to find a job. If you've done a good job of research, you should prepared with a list of skill examples you have that can easily be transferred to the skills that the company needs.

As you prepare for the interview, jot down some ideas that you can discuss about what you did during your career that matches what you think this company may need based on its products and services. Talk about how you think these experiences and skills will make it easy for you to quickly become a valuable employee.

Can You Relate Your Past Experiences to Our Current Business Needs?

When you're changing industries you're likely to be hit with this type of question. As you prepare for the interview, make a list of past experiences that you think are relevant to the industry in which you plan to seek employment or the type of position you are seeking. Compare this list of past experiences with the industry or job you want to move into. Identify any skills you think are relevant and be prepared to discuss how they would meet the needs of the hiring manager.

Don't hesitate to talk about your ability and eagerness to learn new things. Discuss how quickly you learn and how much effort you put into anything you do. If you've taken coursework to prepare for the job change, be sure to discuss it and how that will help meet the new company's needs.

Longevity Questions

Most hiring managers hate the process of hiring people and hope to find candidates who will stick around for a while, so they don't have to go about hiring and training someone again too soon. People over forty or those changing industries may be asked about how long they plan to stay. Expect to be asked and decide how you want to respond to longevity questions before you start interviewing. That way, when the discussion starts your response will sound sincere and well thought out.

I See You've Been Out of Work for a While. Why Is That?

If you've been out of work for about six months or more, don't be hesitant to own up to it. Talk about how you spent your time and point out some activities that make you better qualified for the job, such as training or research. You can also talk about how you wanted to take time off to think about what to do next and, after carefully researching your options, you've chosen to do the type of work for which you're now applying. Talk about your research and make the hiring manager comfortable that you have thought things through and know what you want to do.

Don't ever give the interviewer the indication that you were looking around and this job simply sounded like something you wanted to try out. Be more positive than that and make your reasons for choosing the particular line of work clear and decisive.

If you took time to learn a new skill, that's a great reason to be out of work for a while. Retraining will show the hiring manager how interested you are in the job change. Talk about the skills you've learned and how you believe they will contribute to the company.

You've Moved Around a Lot. Can You Explain?

Your resume may look very spotty because of all the job changes you had to take after losing the career position you had. Be ready to talk about and explain your reasons for your job changes. If you've changed fields or industries, you may want to discuss how you had to work your way back up the ladder, which required job changes to broaden your knowledge or skills. If you changed jobs for promotions, be sure to point that out and how quickly you learned and moved up in your new career.

If it's relevant to your reason for job change, which will probably be the case after a layoff, discuss the economy and how you've had to make changes to meet the challenges of an ever-changing and turbulent economic landscape. Talk about your willingness to learn new industries and new skills to stay competitive through this period of dramatic change.

You can easily change the negative of moving around into a positive about managing and responding to change effectively, but you do have to prepare and practice your response before the interview so it sounds sincere and convincing.

Were You Consulting, or Merely Out of Work?

Many people try to make their resumes look better by filling in a long gap without work with their own consulting business. Hiring managers see it all the time, so be prepared to talk about your consulting work if that is on your resume.

If you were laid off from a full-time position, but continued working for you former company as a consultant so you could complete several ongoing projects, talk about those projects and why the company specifically wanted you to finish them. You should be able to make yourself sound indispensable and build your credibility.

Now that you've finished the projects you're ready to start work on something new and exciting. Talk about how the open position appeals because you are ready for a new challenge.

If you have just used consultant as a resume-filler, you may want to joke about it, but you're better off not trying to hide the fact that you were out of work. Instead talk about what you did do to keep yourself competitive in the marketplace.

Be ready to discuss how you spent your time while unemployed, which could include reading professional journals to keep up on the most current information in your field or maybe to catch up because you just didn't have time to when you were working full time. You may just have been looking for work and be prepared to handle the question without sounding guilty. Know what you want to say because if you have a significant gap on your resume, you will be asked about it.

You've Been at One Company So Long. Can You Adapt to Our Company?

You may be someone who worked all your adult life at one company, or at least for the past ten or twenty years before being laid off. While that makes you look like a very stable person, it also may make you look like you'll have a hard time getting used to a change.

You can handle this type of question in several different ways. One way is just to say that you're looking forward to a change and are eager to do something different. After much research, you've decided this is exactly the right type of position for you. Talk about the research you did and how you came to the decision to seek work in the field for which you are interviewing.

You can also talk about all the changes your former company went through over the years and how you thrived during those change periods. If you led the change during one or more of those periods for your former department or company, be sure to be ready to discuss your change management skills and what you learned about change. This will help to convince the hiring manager that you handle change well and are worth considering for the position you are seeking.

Practice Your Answers with Friends and Family

I'm sure you notice that the most important thing you can do to get ready for the interview is to practice your answers to these tough questions. In addition to these, think of other questions you've been asked on previous interviews. If you were an interviewer in the past, think about the type of questions you asked and why you asked them.

Prepare a response for any question you think you might be asked. You probably will come up with a better answer if you do some research, craft smart answers, and practice your responses until you are comfortable talking about the issue.

You may want to develop a list of the tough questions and then ask family members or friends to use them to do a mock interview. If you'd like and you have the video equipment, record your interview. Then you can watch yourself and improve your responses.

Talking Salary

You should never bring up salary during the interview. If the subject is discussed, it should be initiated by the interviewer. Also, try to avoid being the first person to throw out a figure. Often the interviewer will ask you for your salary range. While you should know that answer, don't volunteer it easily.

As part of your research, you should have found the range for the position to which you are applying, but don't use that information unless you're boxed into a corner. Try deflecting a question about money with a question, such as what is the range that's available for a new hire. If you decide you need to give a number, indicate that according to the research you've done, the market rate for this type of job is such and such and given your level of experience you believe you are in the middle or top of that range. Never sell yourself short.

End of the Interview

One of the best things you can hear at the end of an interview is that you're hired. You likely won't get an offer during the interview; unless this isn't the first time you're meeting with the hiring manager. I have found many large companies only allow the HR staff to make the actual offer to be sure it's done within certain legal guidelines, so don't be surprised if the hiring manager is not the one who calls you with the offer.

If you don't get an offer at the end of an interview, ask what the next steps are in the process. If you're talking to the person who will make the hiring decision, he should give you a timeframe for following up. If they are interviewing more candidates, he'll either escort you to the next stop or let you know when to expect another call.

Don't start to panic if you don't hear anything by the quoted timeframe. Things almost always get in the way—someone gets sick, the hiring manger gets tied up in another emergency, or myriad other things crop up that can create the need for a schedule change.

As soon as you get home, write thank-you notes to everyone you met with during the interview process. Try to focus on one or two points that you think makes you the best candidate for the job and mention them in the note. Be sure you convey your excitement about the potential job.

If you've been waiting more than a week for an answer, call back or send an e-mail to ask how things are going. Don't go on the offensive. Just ask about the new timing for a decision.

You may get the bad news that someone else was offered the position. If that happens, ask if there are other positions open for which they'd consider you. Also ask to be considered for positions that open in the future. Check back on a monthly basis with a quick e-mail to keep your name on top of the list and let the recruiter know you're excited about the prospect of working for that company.

Congratulations!

Finally, after all your hard work, you're hired. You will likely be offered a set salary and benefits. If you've done your homework you should know whether the offer is about right, too low, or too high. Don't worry if the salary offer is higher unless that higher paycheck comes with very few benefits. Than you may want to negotiate for the benefits you need even if the salary will be lower once you beef up the benefits.

If the offer is too low, you'll need to think long and hard about whether you want to accept the position. Raises will be few and far between and most companies are giving raises of only 4 percent or less in this market. So unless the hiring manager indicates that the offer represents a lower initial salary during a probationary period followed by a significant raise, don't jump at a low-ball offer. Ask for more. If you don't get it, you may not want the job. But be realistic. If jobs are scarce you should take it and keep your eyes open for something better.

Now let's take a look at how you should start your new job, as well as what you should do to stay ready for a job search in the future.

RECAP: You may need longer than one week to complete the tasks in this chapter. Don't be discouraged if you need to take longer than a week, but before you move on to Chapter 7, be sure you:

- Practice stress-reduction tips at home so you'll be able to use them effectively while you are waiting for the interview. You'll do much better on the interview if you are calm and composed.
- Develop your checklist, so you'll feel confident when you leave the house that you have everything you need for the interview.
- Practice reading body language with your family and friends, so you can recognize body stances while you are in an interview and be sure you are conveying the right messages with your body position.
- Prepare your answers in writing to both the easy questions *and* the tough questions.

- Practice your answers with family and friends and listen to their feedback. Keep an open mind even if you disagree with them.
- Always write an effective thank-you letter after an interview. You can send the letter by snail mail, but e-mail is usually better, especially if a quick decision is to be made.

- Tips for starting a new job
- Making a great impression
- Keeping up your network

CHAPTER 7

Week 10: You're Hired!

YOU'RE READY TO start your new job but you probably won't yet feel confident. That will come in time. You're probably feeling a mix of emotions—elated to have a new position, nervous about making a good impression, uncertain if you can do a good job, relief that the financial uncertainty is over—and those are just a few of the common emotions people feel when they get a job offer. In this chapter, we'll take a look at what you need to do at your new job, as well as things that will help you stay better prepared if you face another job layoff in the future.

Starting Fresh

When you first start a job, no matter how much experience you'll be bringing to your new position, remember that you are the new kid on the block and even people with fewer years of professional experience know more than you do about the internal politics of the company. Tread carefully, sit back, and watch. Get to know the political dynamics of an organization before you start making any waves or putting your big foot forward. You could end up with proverbial "foot in mouth disease," if you don't walk a very thin line at first.

You want to show that the manager made a good choice in hiring you, so look for things you can do that will make a good impression quickly. Maybe you'll find a task that someone has been struggling with and you have an idea to make it easier to for him or her to complete that task. Gently offer a suggestion and see if the staff person bites. Don't push if the person resists your involvement. You don't know the office politics and you don't want to make waves.

As the new kid on the block, you must show that you can fit into the existing corporate culture. You must avoid upsetting anyone and quickly apologize even if you think you are in the right. While you can offer to help, you may be stepping on someone's untouchable turf or pet project, so be careful where you insert yourself.

You must keep repeating to yourself that the company and its internal workings were there a long time before you (unless of course it's a start-up, but then you must be careful not to step on the egos of the founders). There are established procedures that have been in place for a long time and they were probably established to correct other problems in the past, so your coworkers and managers may not like to hear any suggestions about change. In fact, your suggestion may have been tried and failed in the past. There could be business, personal, political, or technical reasons why the company does something a specific way.

Instead of suggesting anything new, take the time to learn what the company does and why it does it in the way it does. You could discover that the manager who hired you is the one who designed the system and it's his pet project. Suggesting or pushing for changes could destroy any chance you have of making a good impression.

Make a Great Impression Your First Week

So now that I've given you all these warnings, you're probably wondering how to make a good impression your first week. Here are some helpful hints:

> *Stay positive*—a positive and friendly attitude will go a long way to let your new coworkers and bosses know you are excited about the job and glad to be there. Even if after you're there for a day you're disappointed by some things you see, don't reveal it. Let it out at home with family and friends, but don't bring that disappointment into the office. Be sure to let your coworkers know you are team player. If there are any problems at home, financial or otherwise, that cropped up during your period of unemployment, don't let them follow you into the workplace. Use the blocking techniques we discussed in Chapter 6 to keep personal stuff off of your mind during the workday.

> *Dress to fit in*—You want to fit in, but still dress professionally. You don't want to overdress and give the impression that you are an elitist, but even worse you don't want to look sloppy and give a bad impression. If you are perfectly groomed, you will be looked upon as being efficient and reliable. If you walk in looking sloppy, you could give the impression that you are disorganized and untrustworthy.

> *Show you're a team player*—Work with your coworkers. Don't try so hard to make a good impression that your coworkers think you are aloof and reject working as a team. Look for opportunities to solve problems in a group and get the job done. Share recognition with the team, even if you feel you've done all the work. Always be sure you give credit to others who've worked with you.

Learn names quickly—If you're like me and have a hard time learning names, search for memory tricks and see what works for you. You won't be expected to know everyone's name by the end of the first week, but the faster the better to make a good impression. If you do forget someone's name, apologize and ask it again. Don't hide the fact that you don't know the name or you'll never learn names at all.

Ask for help—You're the new kid on the block, so don't feel like you have to figure everything out on your own. Ask others for help when you're unsure about how to do things. You're not expected to know everything during your first week. You're much better off asking for help and getting something done right, than trying to figure things out and doing something wrong. Fixing a mess usually takes longer than answering a question. Your boss will much prefer to take time to answer a question than have to deal with a mess you might make just because you were afraid to ask.

Write things down—Keep a notepad with you and write things down regarding rules of the company and any systems you must follow. By doing that you can review your notes rather than asking the same question over and over again. You will lose credibility fast if you have to keep asking the same questions.

Look for work—As the new kid on the block, you'll probably be given things to do in very small doses to give you a chance to learn the ropes. Don't twiddle your thumbs when you finish the task. Let your boss know you're done and are ready for the next assignment. If your boss is busy, offer to help a coworker until your boss is ready for you.

Arrive early, stay late—To make a good impression you need to show that you are reliable and ready to put in that extra effort. During the first week, try to get to the office about thirty minutes early and stay about thirty minutes later—unless of course your boss tells you to leave on time. Getting there early gives you time to get a cup of coffee and talk to others before the workday starts. If you and the boss are the only ones there, it will give you time to build your relationship with her as well. But, if your boss gets in early to plan the day before staff arrives, be sure you don't interrupt her daily routine. Just being there will show your initiative.

Avoid time off—Working every day for the first week and even the first few months is critical. You want to show you're dependable. Even if an emergency comes up at home try to avoid taking a day off.

Avoid office politics—Every office has politics and you need to understand those politics before you get your feet wet. As the newbie, you're best off avoiding all gossip and politics until you really know the power players. Otherwise, you could get drawn into the clique of the wrong power player and destroy your chances of moving up in the organization. Pick your mentors carefully based on where they are in the organization and where they are going. That could take months to figure out. You definitely won't know enough in the first week or even the first month.

Avoid personal business—While you may have been used to handling personal tasks on company time in the past (such as checking e-mail, buying stuff online, or making reservations for dinner), don't do it during your first week on the job. Carefully observe others' behavior. Also, talk about it with your boss so you understand company policy. Stick to the rules until you feel secure in your new position, which could take several months.

Get involved after hours—If your company has activities you can join after hours, such as a sports league, join in. It's a great way to get to know your coworkers and show that you are a team player. Do exercise caution if drinking takes place at these after-hour activities. You don't want to say or do something stupid just because you've had one too many! Drink moderately anytime you are out with coworkers.

Become a great listener—As the rookie, you know nothing. Think of yourself as a sponge absorbing everything around you, but don't squeeze out what you've learned until you feel secure that you know the company and its culture.

Say thanks—Be sure you don't forget to say thanks to anyone who helps you. Showing your appreciation makes them want to continue to help.

Be sure you keep your boss informed about what you are doing. She may set up regular training times during the first week. If not, try to find times where you can grab her for a few minutes to review what you've been doing. Make sure it's what she wants you to focus on and ask what she wants you to work on next. Your boss may have laid out a week of training-type tasks. If so, just stop by briefly and let her know where you are on the list and ask any questions that might have come up as you were working.

Continue Networking

You've started to build a great network of professional support so don't let that network go just because you've landed a job. After you're settled into your new position, make contact with your networking buddies; let them know where you landed and what you're doing. Indicate you'd like to stay in touch with them. You enjoyed their insights on various topics (mention a few that you think interest them most) and you'd like to meet for lunch periodically to exchange ideas. Also let them know they shouldn't hesitate to contact you if there is anything you can do for them in the future.

Your network isn't done. Continue building it even as you get settled in the new job. You'll be meeting lots of new networking buddies as you make contact with people inside and outside the new company. A network is a living and breathing organism that constantly needs to be fed and nurtured to remain an effective tool for the future.

Your Career Path

Once you get settled in your new job start thinking about how this position fits on your career path. If you've changed industries or career paths, ask yourself whether you need additional training in order to go further. With a career change this is commonly the case.

Look for opportunities to learn more and find out your new company's policy regarding footing the bill for education. Most companies won't pay for training until you've been with the company for a year, but if you need certain certifications, coursework may be part of your initial training period. For example, if you're hired as a financial advisor, it's common for the company to pay for courses so you can pass the tests and receive your required certifications and licenses.

RECAP: You'll most likely need more time than just one week to complete the tasks in this chapter. Here's what you need to accomplish this week and for all the years you're on your new job:

- Be sure to handle yourself cautiously as you start work at the new job. Take time to observe office politics to be sure you don't step on the wrong toes.
- Make a great first impression by showing good work habits and staying positive.
- Keep building your network and be sure to say thanks to those who helped you during your job search. Also, be ready to give back if others in your network need help.

- Reassessing your finances for the long haul
- Considering short-term positions
- Developing a business plan

CHAPTER 8

Long-Term Unemployment

YOU'VE SPENT MONTHS looking for employment and nothing is clicking. It's time to think about putting a Plan B into place to help you get to where you want to be in your career. In this chapter, we'll discuss coping with the stress and depression of being out of work, getting your financial situation squared away, as well as how to go about drumming up short-term contract or consulting work. Who knows? You might even decide to start your own business—we'll get into the basics of that as well.

You've done all the right stuff: You've worked through the anger and depression of your layoff, told family and friends, pulled together your life plan and career goals, networked, sent out your resumes, and made follow-up calls.

And nothing happens.

Sometimes, because of a severe downturn in the economy, doing all the right things to get a job isn't enough. Sometimes, your unemployment, which you thought would only last a few months, stretches on and on. When that happens, you need to employ some of the same coping mechanisms you used right after losing your job. It's important that you not sink back into depression and inactivity, or your long-term unemployment could become permanent. Here are some things you should work on:

It's not you. When employers are not responding to your resumes and applications, you may start to take it personally. Don't. In nine out of ten cases, companies either aren't hiring at all or they're being extremely selective about who they hire. In any case, it's not personal, so don't take it as a comment about you.

Make sure it's not you. While not taking it personally, if you're not getting any response from the companies to which you're applying, it's a good idea to check your resume and references. Look for anything that might be a red flag to potential employers. Are there any unexplained gaps or other hiccups in the resume that stand out? Are your references giving you good recommendations? Talk to them and make sure. Show your resume to the people in your network and get their opinion. If they were employers, would they consider hiring you? Tell them to be objective and honest—you need to know if something's getting in the way of your job prospects.

Reach out. Long-term unemployment can be discouraging, but this isn't the time to isolate yourself. Contact your friends, family, and others who are part of your network. Stay connected to them, and ask them for support. They'll give it to you, and it will sustain you during this difficult period.

Watch the news. Especially if the economy's in a downturn that's created your job-seeking difficulties, pay attention to the state of affairs in the business world. You want to be poised, when an upturn happens, to take full advantage of it.

Look at which companies seem to be weathering the storm, and watch for employment prospects there.

Enhance your skill set. Months of unemployment shouldn't mean months of idleness. This is your chance to improve your marketability. Check into business classes or other sorts of classes offered at the local community college. Get some books from the library and learn some new computer programs. Practice your writing and speaking skills. The more skills you can list on your resume, the more attractive you are to companies.

Keep a schedule. This is one of the hardest things to do, but it's among the most important. Even when week after week and month after month goes by without a nibble on your job line, you need to stick to a routine. Get up at the same time in the morning, dress neatly, and, after a good breakfast, get to work. Don't sleep late or slop around the house in sweats or an old pair of pajama bottoms. That can deepen your depression and sense of failure. Plan out your day and your week in advance, including some time for exercise to clear your mind. And stick to that plan, no matter what.

If the situation goes on long enough, it may be necessary to take some sort of job—any job—just to keep money coming into the household. If that's the case, approach that job with the same level of professionalism with which you'd approach your dream career. After all, you don't know how long you'll have to work as a clerk at the corner convenience store or unloading boxes down at the depot. Impress your boss and she or he may become a valuable part of your network, telling you about career opportunities when they occur.

Long-term unemployment is always stressful. But it doesn't have to be fatal to your career.

Preparing for a Long Spell of Joblessness

If you've come to the conclusion that your job search will require a long period of joblessness, you also need to prepare yourself financially. Look back at your numbers from the first week after the layoff. Is your budget working? How much do you have left in the bank? Have you already had to approach family or friends for money?

You need to reassess your financial position for the long haul and will likely need to figure out how to get cash flowing even if it means doing work you might not want to do. You need to pay for housing, food, and medical care. So even if it means taking a job near minimum wage, bite the bullet. You can probably find a job paying better than minimum wage by signing up with several temporary job placement agencies. If you have a technical specialty, such as accounting or computer programming, you should be able to find temporary work at wages near what you were earning in the past, minus the benefits you enjoyed.

But before you do that, think about your skill set. Can they be used to work for someone temporarily as a freelancer or independent contractor? Do you have the expertise to be hired as a consultant? If so, you should consider working for yourself.

First Steps

Before you can start looking for freelance, contract or consulting work, you must structure your business day. Hopefully you've done a good job of setting up an office and establishing a routine during your job search. But now you have to start thinking about this as a long-term situation. After you get some contracts in place and are earning money, you may want to think about renting office space outside the home if working at home is a problem, but you likely won't have the money to do that right away.

Restructure your day as a nine–to–five workday, even if you actually work 5 A.M. to 2 P.M. and then spend your afternoon with family. The great thing about being your own boss is that you set your work hours. The only limits on the hours you set may be related to the contracts you win. When you do get a contract you may have to adjust your work hours to meet the needs of your client.

Project-Based Work

Freelance or independent contractor work involves getting work on a project-by-project basis. If you have writing skills you may be able to set up freelance assignments with a magazine or newspaper. Or, you may be able to work as an independent contractor helping a company to get a website set up or put out a publication. A freelance assignment is usually very short term, while an independent contract position could extend for a longer period of time. Many independent contractors are almost like employees, but they don't get the benefits, so if you are hired as a freelancer or independent contractor be sure you truly do have the independence you want and the company is not just using that terminology to avoid paying benefits.

In this case I'm not only talking about health and other insurance benefits, I'm also talking about Social Security, Medicare, and other employer taxes that can be avoided with an independent contractor agreement. For example, when 6.2 percent of your pay is taken out as an employee for Social Security, your employer matches the same percentage. If you're an independent contractor you must pay the full 12.4 percent. In addition to that you must pay both the employer and employee costs for Medicare which totals 2.9 percent. So as an independent contractor, 15.3 percent of your net income will be paid to Uncle Sam at tax time. It won't be taken out of your check. You'll need to make quarterly payments toward estimated taxes.

As an independent contractor, you should be able to set your own schedule, decide where you want to work, and decide how you want to do that work provided you can meet the specifications of the contract. Your contract should specify that you are hired on a project-by-project basis. Your duties should be carefully spelled out. You must put in writing which party will be responsible for materials, supplies, and other items that may be needed to complete the project. If you think you may need assistants to get the project done on time or you want to subcontract some of the work, you must spell that out and be sure the costs are specified in the contract as well.

The IRS knows employers use the independent contractor status as a way to avoid paying taxes, so they have developed a twenty-question test. Take the test and see if you are truly being hired as an independent contractor. If not, you may actually be an employee and entitled to employee's benefits. If you think you qualify as an employee after taking this test, you can file Form SS-8 (*www.irs.gov/pub/irs-pdf/fss8.pdf*): "Determination of Worker Status for Purposes of Federal Employment Taxes and Income Tax Withholding." If the IRS rules in your favor, your employer could be required to pay back the employer's share of Medicare and Social Security taxes as well as compensate you for the benefits you didn't, but should have received during the time you worked for them. Here's the twenty-question test:

1. *Is the worker allowed to perform services for a number of clients at the same time?* You should be able to answer yes to this question. If the company that hired you doesn't allow you to work for others you are not an independent contractor. This does not mean you must work

for more than one company at a time, only that you should have the option to do so.

2. *Are the worker's services regularly available to the general public?* You must be able to answer yes. You should be able to advertise your services, maintain a visible office and business phone listing and be available to offer your services to others.

3. *Does the agreement prevent the worker from doing gainful work during the period of the agreement?* You should be able to answer no to this question. As an independent contractor you must be free to work for as many companies as you want.

4. *Can the worker establish his or her own hours?* You must be able to set your own work hours, as long as you can meet the deadlines established in the independent contractor agreement.

5. *Has the worker invested in facilities and/or equipment to perform?* As an independent contractor you usually work at your own facilities using equipment you own.

6. *Will a significant portion of the work be done at the company's facilities?* You should be able to answer no to this question. A majority of your work should be done at your own place of work, not at the company offices.

7. *Will the worker receive training from the company?* The answer to this question should be no. If you are being hired as an independent contractor it means you know how to do the work that is needed. You should not need training for the job.

8. *If assistants are needed, will these be provided by the company?* You should be able to answer no to this question, unless it is specified in this contract that you will be hiring assistants to be paid as part of the contract fee. Even in this case the fee should be paid to you and you should pay the assistants as your employees.

9. *Does a continuing relationship for an ongoing task exist?* Your contract should not be open ended on time. You should have a clearly defined relationship that ends when you complete the work specified in the terms of the contract.

10. *Will the company determine the order or sequence of the tasks to be completed?* You should answer no to this question. As an independent contractor you should be able to complete the tasks in the manner that you find most efficient as long as you produce the desired results.

11. *Can the worker realize the economic loss for nonperformance other than the loss of payment for personal services?* You should be able to answer yes to this question. Your services should be provided for a flat fee. If you have any nonrelated expenses that are not specified as reimbursable, you can take a loss based on these expenses. So when you draft the contract be certain you take all possible expenses into consideration.

12. *Is a progress report or timesheet required for a performance evaluation?* You should be able to answer no to this question. A company can't require you to clock in everyday, but it can require infrequent progress reports to be sure you're staying on track to meet the deadlines.

13. *Will the worker be paid on an hourly basis?* The answer to this questions should be no. An independent contractor is paid by the project. You should set an established fee for the project no matter how many hours it takes you to complete.

14. *Will the worker be reimbursed for incidentals (expenses related to the services performed)?* You should be able to answer no to this question. As a contractor you are responsible for all expenses necessary to complete the job, except for those expenses specified in the contract.

15. *Will the company furnish tools other than specialized equipment?* You should be able to answer no to this question. As an independent contractor you are expected to supply and maintain the tools or equipment you need to complete the job. There can be exception for this if some of the tools or equipment you must use are unique to the company that hired you.

16. *Is the worker required to comply with instructions other than general project parameters?* Your answer to this question should be no. Your instructions should be laid out in the general project parameters as specified in the contract. You cannot be micromanaged by the person who hired you.

17. *Does the success of the project hinge on performance of the work?* Your answer to this should be no. You should be supporting the general work of the company but your work can not be a determining factor in the success or failure of the company. If that is the case then the company would likely want to exert more control over what you do.

18. *Must services be rendered personally?* You should be able to answer no. As an independent contractor you're hired to get a project done. If it's more efficient for you to complete the project on time by hiring an assistant you should be allowed to do it as long as the work performed meets the standards set in the contract.

19. *Can the worker be discharged for convenience as one would an hourly employee, as opposed to discharge related to contract requirements?* You can't be fired like an hourly employee as long as you produce according to the terms of the contract. All independent contractor contracts should specify how work can be terminated and how compensation should be calculated if the work is terminated early.

20. *Can the worker unilaterally terminate the contract prior to completion?* You cannot terminate a contract without getting agreement from the company that hired you. You are legally obligated to complete the work as promised. If you don't, you can be sued for breach of contract.

Taking on contract work can be a good way to bring in extra cash, but do remember you are signing a legal document and if something goes wrong you can end up in a courtroom. So don't enter into this type of agreement without careful consideration of what you are promising to do and how much you need to be paid to cover your costs as well as make a profit.

Consulting in Your Industry

If you'd like to earn extra money in between jobs after you've been laid off, you may want to consider setting up a consulting business. If you've worked fifteen to twenty years in a particular field or have a particular skill that a lot of people need, you may be able to make it as a consultant. But it's up to you to package and sell yourself as an expert, so other people will want to buy your services.

You will find that you take on many different roles as a consultant, such as:

- Problem-solver—You help a company sort out a problem and come up with a solution.
- Detective—You figure out what the problem is and how it can be corrected.
- Wise Man—You review decisions that have already been made and validate them.
- Counselor—You help to figure out what is getting in the way of a company's success. If you decide to work with

small businesses, you almost become a therapist for the business owner.

- Facilitator—You help a company achieve its goal. For example, you could be called in to improve financial reporting if your specialty is in the financial management area.

Can You Make It as a Consultant?

Consultants are needed in many areas. Search online using the word "consulting." You will find consultants in the fields of advertising, technology, construction, design, entertainment, financial services, law, politics, resume building, theater, telecommunication, and dozens of other areas.

Your only limit is the experience and knowledge you bring to the table. Before someone will pay the big bucks to hire you as a consultant, you have to prove your worth to them based on your knowledge and skills.

You're probably wondering what skills you need. Your skills must have fall into three categories—technical skills, project skills, and personal skills.

- Technical Skills—Skills you need for your specialty, such as accounting, writing, or whatever area you've been working in for the past fifteen to twenty years.
- Project Skills—Skills you'll need to manage a project, such as creating the product, client service skills, interviewing, negotiating, presenting recommendations, problem-identification, problem-solving, proposal development, team building, and time management.
- Personal Skills—Skills you'll need to develop personally so you can sell yourself and do the work, such as collaboration, communications, interpersonal, leadership, listening, management, marketing, and promotional.

If you think you may be weak in any of these skill sets, you may want to find a partner for your consulting work. All these skills are needed by a consultant at one time or another.

How Do Consultants Work?

Basically consultants are hired to solve a problem. As a consultant, it's your job to figure out what's gone wrong or what needs to be done. Most consultants solve the problem by working through these five major steps:

1. *Problem Investigation*—Talk with people in the company. Then, research information and collect data so you'll be able to analyze the problem. Use your past experiences to recognize weaknesses and figure out who you need to talk with about the problem. You will likely be able to recognize who may be protecting their turf and who may be creating resistance to the solution. You'll need to talk with the key people blocking the solution to get their side of the story. Don't assume your solution is right until you've done a full investigation. Remember you want to look at this from a fresh prospective and not just the prospective you might have had while working for your former company.

2. *Data Analysis*—Next, you need to analyze the problem to figure out the causes and symptoms. For example, suppose as you start your research regarding the manufacture of the new product, you find the line manager has some serious concerns about how it will fit in the production line. The manufacturing manager might have decided that the new product cannot easily be built alongside other products in the line. Your solution may be that you recommend outsourcing the manufacturing. You'd then need to collect all the pros

and cons about outsourcing the new product and how it will impact the bottom line.

3. *Make Recommendations*—Once you finish your analysis, develop a set of recommendations that answer the questions posed by the person or people in the company when they hired you for the project. For example, if your task was to fix the manufacturing problems on the line for a new product, discuss the roadblocks you found and recommend how you think the company can fix the problem. As an outside consultant, you should be prepared with recommendations for how to handle any objections you heard from various department heads during your investigation.

4. *Develop Your Plan to Fix the Problem*—In addition to recommendations, you'll also need to come up with a plan for how the company can manage the change you are recommending. For example, if during your investigation and analysis of the manufacturing, you find you need to recommend outsourcing as a solution, you could find yourself in the role of advocating outsourcing. The company may want you to be involved in managing the changeover to outsourcing. If that's the case, then this would be considered an additional project. You would need to negotiate an extension of the contract to do the work necessary to implement the change.

5. *Implement Your Recommendations*—Sometimes your contract may include provisions for implementation of your recommendations. For example, you could be asked to spearhead the manufacture and introduction of the new product. Once the product is launched, you would pass the day-to-day operations to a manufacturing manager and a product manager who are full-time employees. These people would probably be working with you throughout implementation of the project.

You may find it hard to bid a contract for implementation prior to your final recommendations being accepted, so be sure to protect yourself with a clause for negotiating hours and fees once the recommendations have been accepted and you know exactly what work will be required.

No matter what type of consulting work you do, you must learn to listen. You should never do too much of the talking, especially when you're in the phase of the project where you're collecting information and developing your recommendations. In order to collect information effectively, you should say as little as possible and instead encourage people to talk.

Even when you initially meet with the client before the project begins, your listening skills will be critical to your success. You must listen to what your client wants to accomplish by hiring you as a consultant. It's also critical that you ask the right questions and listen carefully to the answers. You certainly don't want to put in hours on a contract only to find out that the finished product of the contract doesn't satisfy the original scope of the task or meet the needs of the company. You're wasting your time and the time of the people who hired you if you don't listen carefully right up front.

Build a Network

In order to be successful you must have an extensive network of contacts. Your initial network will be former coworkers and vendors with whom you worked before you were laid off. You'll probably be able to win a few projects to get your consulting business off the ground directly from people in this network, but to be successful as a consultant you'll need to continue to work on growing this network.

A good place to find networking contacts in your area will be the local Chamber of Commerce. Make an appointment with a member of the membership committee or the membership staff person to talk about the various business groups that operate through the chamber. Plan to volunteer with at least one of these groups that handle issues relating to the type of work you want to do as a consultant. You'll meet and work with people that ultimately can help you build your network.

Another good source for networking is Business Network International (BNI). BNI's entire purpose is to offer its business and professional members the opportunity to share ideas, contacts and most importantly, referrals. You probably can find a local chapter near you. Visit BNI's website (*www.bni .com*) to locate the nearest chapter and find out more about the organization.

Networking to build a consulting business is somewhat more complex than career networking. You don't just want a bunch of introductions; you need to get people to want to recommend you. So it will take time to truly build a consulting network. Don't expect success overnight. Here are some steps you'll need to take to get known:

Meet potential contacts—Start by calling people whose business cards you collected at a party or other business function. Jot down a few notes regarding your conversation on the back of the card so you remember your conversation and so that you have a good reason to call. Do this as soon as possible after the conversation so you don't end up with a bunch of cards but no idea who's attached to each or what you talked about. I know this can be difficult during a business function, but you likely will forget some key details if you don't find a quiet, inconspicuous place to jot down some key points on each card, even if it means slipping into the bathroom periodically.

Set up a "get to know you" meeting—When you call, remind them of where you met and mention what you talked about. Then set up a time to meet them for coffee or lunch so you can continue your discussion. If they mentioned a problem, volunteer to discuss some tips for how they can handle that problem if relates to your specialty. Don't push to start working with them right away unless the conversation naturally flows in that direction. Remember this first meeting is a "get to know you" session, not a sales session. If you come on too strong you may never get to the next steps, which permit you to build a long-lasting relationship.

Become a known entity—Let the friendship grow naturally. As you get to know each other, if the relationship is going to work for you, you must mutually decide you want to spend time together. Only then can you start building a business relationship. People do business with other people with whom they feel comfortable working. You want to get into your potential client's comfort zone.

When you're trying to get into someone's comfort zone, do a lot of listening and ask a lot of questions. You must show you are truly interested in the other person and his or her business. By listening, you'll find out a lot more about the other person and how you might help them. As you talk, offer simple tips or solutions to build up your credibility with your potential client.

As your friendship grows and you become a known entity, the person may mention you to someone else, but they may not yet be comfortable enough to recommend you. At that point they'll feel comfortable telling others about your expertise and background, but may not be ready to put their reputation on the line by encouraging someone else to work with you.

When your contact finally feels comfortable enough to highly recommend you to others, you've got a strong addition to your network. At this point your contact helps to sell you. You probably won't get to this point until you've actually done one or two projects for your contact. You may be able to get there more quickly by helping them out of a few quick binds and offering tips or advice during a lunch or telephone conversation.

Don't forget to keep in contact with those who have known you for years. Be sure to let them know that you're planning to start a consulting business. They can't help you if they don't know what you plan to do!

Non-Compete Clauses

When you accepted your severance package, you probably were required to sign a non-compete clause. This could limit your ability to consult for companies that compete with your former company for six months. If you did sign a non-compete clause, be sure that you were compensated for signing that clause, especially if you were considering starting your own consulting business after the layoff.

If you signed the clause already and decided to start a consulting business several weeks or months after being laid off, you will have to live with it, but take it to an attorney for review. Each state has its own set of rules about how non-compete clauses can be written. Sometimes companies write clauses that are really not enforceable.

Even if you refused to sign your company's non-compete clause, the company can take you to court to prevent you from working for a competitor or starting your own business.

Whether or not your company's non-compete and non-disclosure agreements are legal and binding depends on the laws in your state or locality. If you do decide to consult for a competitor, be sure you understand your company's agreements as well as the state laws governing those agreements.

In many states, non-compete and non-disclosure agreements are legal. While these states don't want to restrict employees from earning a living, their laws tend to protect companies as long as the agreements are reasonable in scope and necessary to protect the company's business interests. Common restrictions allowed include that you can't work for a competitor for six months or within a twenty-five or fifty miles radius of the company.

But if your job ended because your employer laid you off, the non-compete clause may not hold up in court. Courts do tend to side with the employee if the employer terminated the employment and it was not the employee's fault.

Another issue that could come up if you are being challenged on a non-compete clause could be the compensation you received for signing the non-compete agreement. For example, if you signed a non-compete agreement that restricted your working for a competitor for six months and part of that agreement was that you were paid six-months income as severance, the court will likely consider that reasonable compensation and uphold your company's non-compete clause.

In some cases employers will ask you to sign a non-compete clause even if it's not enforceable in your state. This can be an intimidation tactic, so be sure to check with an attorney if you sign a non-compete clause and decide later you want to break it. Companies that use this tactic count on the fact that employees don't know the law and, in fear, will abide by the provisions of a non-compete agreement when they leave a job even if they don't have to do so.

Picking Your Specialty

You may have lots of different experiences that you could develop into a consulting business. It's important to define your consulting business around one or two specialty areas in which you can truly sell yourself.

As you review your background, pick out things that you accomplished that you believe are unique or groundbreaking in your industry. You must be careful not to trade company confidential information. Not only could you get sued, but you also will lose a lot of respect and trust among other companies.

Determine Your Prices

Pricing yourself can be difficult. You must carefully balance your need to earn a certain amount of money to cover your expenses and make a profit with your ability to stay competitive and not price yourself out of the market.

If you've done a good job of developing your reputation as a specialist, your ability to set your price high is greatly improved. Companies that know you can get the job done based on projects you've already done for them or based on strong recommendations they've gotten from others will be more willing to pay you top dollar.

You likely will set your rate differently with each type of consulting opportunity. In some cases you may find it best to charge an hourly rate (especially if you're required to attend a lot of meetings at the company); in others, you may quote a daily rate. You also may want to set a rate for an entire project, regardless of the number of hours you spent.

Whatever rate you set, you want to be sure you cover all your expenses and time, as well as leave room for profit. You should also specify carefully what is included in the price and what expenses you will bill for separately. For example, if part of the project involves a significant amount of travel, you should set up your contract to bill those travel expenses separately.

You can also set a monthly retainer fee, once you have developed a strong working relationship with the company. Your retainer fee would guarantee your availability to the company for a certain number of hours per month. If you work more than that set number of hours, you would then include an hourly or daily rate for the time spent working for that company beyond the retainer fee guarantee.

Drafting a Contract

Sit down with an attorney once you've picked your niche and established your fee structure. You won't use the exact same contract for all clients, but you will find that there are many basic clauses that can be used with minor adjustments for each consulting job you take.

Remember, the primary purpose of a contract is to protect yourself and the earnings you expect to receive from your clients. While verbal agreements can sometimes hold up in court if someone doesn't pay you, it's very hard to prove what was agreed to verbally. It's best to put everything in writing before you get started. How detailed your contract will need to be depends on the type of consulting business you plan to run and the type of clients you'll be working with. You may find that a two- or three-page letter of agreement will suffice or your attorney may recommend that you work with something more extensive to protect your interests.

Use the opportunity to build a relationship with an attorney you can call on for any emergencies. You can meet with the attorney periodically to review any problems you've had during the year and possible adjustments to your standard contract or the way you do business. Attorneys can help you:

Decide upon and set up your business structure, which will likely be a sole proprietorship (one owner) or partnership. But if you think you have a great risk of being sued you may want to consider establishing yourself as a limited liability company (LLC) or a corporation. As you discuss your business plans with your attorney, he can advise what might be best for you.

Advise you on regulations that could affect your business and assist you with filing paperwork for necessary licenses, permits, or registrations. If you plan to work out of your home, you need to be sure that you understand any limitations to doing so depending on homeowner association covenants or local ordinances.

Advise you on what types of business insurance you may need and possibly even refer you to a good agent.

Assist you if you have problems collecting from a client. Sometimes a letter from your lawyer can be enough incentive to pay, avoiding a more costly collection battle.

Advise you on how to avoid possible lawsuits as a consultant and defend you in court if it becomes necessary. Hopefully by working with an attorney long before you face any problems, you'll have the skills and knowledge to minimize any hostilities and avoid a costly lawsuit.

Depending on your type of consulting business, you may find it useful to hire an attorney on retainer, so you have someone to call on in an emergency who knows your business. The best way to find an attorney is through referrals from friends and associates who run their own businesses. Another good source for recommendations is the local Chamber of Commerce.

Getting Business

You will find yourself writing proposals frequently in order to get business, but before you even start writing, be sure you understand the scope of the project and what your client wants to achieve. Companies usually call in consultants when they have a major problem and no one inside the company knows how to fix it.

Most times you'll be writing a proposal in answer to a formal request for proposals (RFP). Don't just count on what's in that request. Set up an appointment with the person in charge of the proposal process or someone that person designates. After reviewing the RFP, prepare some incisive questions about the project to get ready for the appointment. While you're meeting with the company representative, gather as much information as you can about the company's expectations. The more you know, the stronger your proposal will be. Use this meeting to establish rapport with one of the decisions makers.

Start your written response to a request for proposal with a brief summary of what the client wants. Then develop one or two attention-getting sentences that make the potential client want to read the rest of your proposal.

Don't try to get creative with your response. Follow the guidelines laid out in the RFP. The company designs these instructions based on how they will rate the proposals. If your proposal is not set up to meet those guidelines, you could be knocked out of the game for not following directions. If they must try to figure out where you answer certain provisions of the request for proposal, you make it too hard for them to compare your proposals to others, so they'll likely just give up on you.

In must cases, you'll find a list of specific tasks that must be done as part of the project. The company will also specify what must be accomplished with each task. As you write your proposal, be sure to use these tasks as heads for each section of your response. Make it as easy for them to find the information as possible.

Companies need to know about your relevant experience and expertise. Include that information in a brief paragraph when writing a short proposal. If you become one of the final candidates you will likely then be asked for a more detailed discussion of your expertise and experience.

You'll also be asked to specify your fees. You probably don't want to talk money too early in the process, but you could come up with some line that gives a range of fees depending upon what is needed. This gives you a lot of negotiating room at the time of final contract.

Develop a Business Plan

If you do decide to start a consulting business, develop a business plan that lays out the business strategy for your own company. Figure out the mission for your business and set its goals so you know where you'd like it to go and how you'll get there. Define your business's niche and clearly detail the knowledge and experience that makes you an expert in that field. You'll need to be able to talk about that briefly when you talk with someone, so develop something that you can easily repeat to prospective clients. You may want to develop a ten-second response, a fifteen-second response and a thirty-second response, so you can answer effectively in any situation. Let the client ask for the details he or she wants after that brief introduction.

Once you've defined your business and how you want to sell yourself, decide what your ideal client might look like. Also write down how you would recognize a potential client when you meet him and figure out what you might use to draw your ideal client to doing business with you.

Now you're ready to begin building your network to get your consulting business off the ground! If consulting isn't quite right for you, but you like the idea of being your own boss, in the following chapter, we'll explore other types of businesses you can start.

RECAP: It'll likely take much longer than one week to complete the tasks in this chapter. Don't be discouraged if it takes a month or more to launch your consulting business, but do focus on these tasks if you find yourself out of work for a longer period of time:

- Reassess your financial position and figure out what you need to do to make it through a long stretch of unemployment financially.
- Think about taking short-term freelance assignments, contract work, or consulting work.
- When building a consulting business, be sure to develop a business plan.

CHAPTER 9

Do You *Really* Want to Go Back to the Rat Race?

AFTER BEING OUT of work for a while, you may decide you just don't want to go back into that rat race. You also don't want to put yourself back on the chopping block and risk getting laid off the next time there's a downturn in the market. You may think you can do a lot better as your own boss and harbor a desire to start your own company.

If you've never thought of starting your own business and you have no idea what you want to do, this is probably not a good option for you. But if you've been dreaming about being your own boss and you know exactly what type of business you want to start, your layoff may be just the impetus you needed. In this chapter we'll explore what it takes to be your own boss and what it takes to run your own business.

Be Your Own Boss

Don't even think about starting a new business from scratch unless you have the financial resources on hand to fund the business for a year as well as pay for your personal needs. New businesses are rarely profitable in their first year. In fact, in most new businesses it can take up to five years before you can count on seeing cash returns. Now that's the rule, but people have proved it wrong.

If you just don't have the time to wait for a new business to get off the ground, you may want to consider buying an existing business, which could be a very good option if you received a significant lump sum as part of your severance package. One of my friends used his severance package to buy a business after he was laid off for the third time. He got a year's severance pay because the company wanted him to agree to a strict non-compete clause for a year. He used that money to buy his dream business and it's flourishing now just three years later.

A third option is to buy into a franchise. These are sometimes called buying a business in a box. The buy-in costs can range from just a few thousand dollars to millions depending on the type of franchise you buy. We'll take a look at all three options, but first let's take a quick look at the help that's available to you.

You don't have to try to start a business alone. Here are resources you can count on if you want to start a small business:

Free Courses—The Small Business Administration offers an extensive array of free courses for small business owners. At its website (*www.sba.gov/training*), you'll find courses to help get you started, focusing on everything from business management, business planning tools, cyber security, e-commerce, financing, government contracting, marketing and advertising, risk management, and taxation. In addition, the website has links to an extensive online business library, national training events, and online university and college business courses.

Service Corps of Retired Executives (SCORE)—SCORE (*www .score.org*) provides you with retired executives who offer their volunteer services to business owners. They'll help you develop your business plan and help you find funding for it.

Small Business Development Centers (SBDCs)—The SBA administers the Small Business Development Center Program (*www.sba.gov/sbdc*) as a cooperative effort among the private sector; the educational community; and federal, state, and local governments. By working with an SBDC, you can get needed management and technical assistance. There are sixty-three lead SBDCs in the country with at least one in every state, the District of Columbia, Guam, Puerto, Samoa, and the U.S. Virgin islands. These lead SBDCs support a network of more than 1,100 service locations that can be found at chambers of commerce, colleges, economic development corporations, and vocational schools. Each center develops services in cooperation with the local SBA district offices to ensure statewide coordination with other available resources.

Women's Business Centers—If you're a woman and want to start your own company, the SBA also provides a network of educational centers designed to assist women start and grow small businesses. WBCs operate to level the playing field for female entrepreneurs who still face unique obstacles in the world of business. To find the WBC in your state go to *www .sba.gov/idc/groups/public/documents/sba_program_office/sba_pr_ wbc_ed.pdf*. You can find out more about this entrepreneurial program at *www.sba.gov/aboutsba/sbaprograms/onlinewbc*.

Launching a New Business from Scratch

Before you even think about asking for help, you must be able to answer these two questions: "What do I want to sell?" and "Who would want to buy it from me?" If you have a business dream in mind, you'll probably find it easy to answer the first question, "What do I want to sell?" but you may find it much hard to answer the second question, "Who would want to buy it from me?"

As you try to answer that second question, make a list of the unique skills and services you might offer in conjunction with the product you want to sell. Try to make your product or service stand out in people's minds. You may hate the idea of writing a business plan, but if you take the time to put it down on paper, it will help you think through what you want to do and improve the success of your business.

Think about these key points as you try to develop your business plan:

Develop a detailed description of your business idea and why you think this idea makes sense given the current market conditions. Don't only think about your great idea as you sort this out. Be sure to look at the competition you'll face, as well as the state of the economy.

Sort out your start-up finances. Be sure you estimate how much money you'll need to get your business started and operate it during the first year. You certainly don't want to get started with a great idea just to find out six months down the road you can't afford to keep it going.

Figure out when you think you can recover your initial investment and when you think the business will return a reasonable profit. You need to estimate initial sales and project sales growth, then subtract any expenses you expect for running the business, including buying your products, marketing and advertising, and administrative expenses.

Develop a list of challenges you expect to face as you start your business. Then figure out a plan for how you will overcome the challenges and make your business a success.

If you've never developed a business plan before, I highly recommend that you take the online business-planning course at *www.sba.gov/smallbusinessplanner/plan/writeabusinessplan*.

Marketing Your Business

As part of the initial planning phase you should determine how to market your business. Start by doing a market and industry analysis:

Describe the market for your proposed product or service. Detail the research you conducted related to the size of your market, the number of potential customers for your product or service, and your projected growth rates for your business, as well as the industry in which you plan to operate.

Review your competition. Determine which companies currently offer products or services similar to what you plan to offer. Remember, the customer seeks a product to solve a problem. Think about the problem you'll be solving and then think how you can help them solve the problem in a different way. For example, people want to communicate with their friends and family. They can do that by using cell phones, e-mail, web-enabled phones, or a traditional telephone service. So if you are thinking of selling a web-enabled phone service, you must remember that the customer won't only be looking at your phone service versus other phones services, he or she also will consider other options for talking with his family and friends. So don't limit your review of competition too narrowly. Think of what you plan to provide that the customer wants and all the ways the customer may be able to satisfy that desire.

Grade your competition. As you collect information about your competition, take note of what's working and what's not. Pick up the good ideas and improve on the bad ones as you develop your own marketing plans. Tread carefully though because you don't want to infringe on trademarks or copyrights. You could be stuck with large legal bills defending yourself if you use something you shouldn't. For example, you can promote add-on services a similar company offers, but you can't use that company's marketing logo (or trademark) and you can't copy their advertising designs.

Funding Your Business

After you've collected all the information you need to detail your product or service, determined what it will cost to offer the product or service, analyzed your competition, projected sales, and designed marketing plans, you're ready to figure out how much money you need to get started. Use this information to develop a budget for the first year and project out a five-year budget.

Your budget should be as truthful as you can make it, but it doesn't have to be carved in stone. Even well-established companies draw up budgets each year and need to make adjustments during the year if market conditions change.

Use this initial budget to sort out how your business will operate and how much money you'll need during the first year. You need to take a stab at analyzing your cash flow and where it will come from in order to have any chance of success. Many businesses fail in the first two years because they do not accurately project their cash flow needs and run out of money. In fact, it's the second most common reason for failure. The number-one reason is poor management.

Without the money you need to market and sell your product, as well as pay any staff or consultants you might need to hire, your business can't succeed. Before it even gets off the ground you may need to cut back and may not be able to market the business appropriately. That will only hasten its demise. You can't sell a product or service without marketing it. Yet many businesses in trouble start cutbacks by skimping on marketing.

If you plan to start from home, your start-up costs will be much less than if you lease retail or other commercial space. If you can start the business with your spouse as your partner and put off hiring staff until your business starts earning enough money, you can reduce your funding needs.

If you do need to raise funds from others to get your business started, here are the possible sources you can tap:

Personal Savings: If all of your savings is tied up as part of a retirement nest egg don't put that savings at risk on one business idea. Remember the adage, "Don't put all your eggs in one basket." Starting a new business is a high-risk venture. Retirement savings is not the type of money you should invest in such a high-risk venture. Rather than take out your retirement funds, you may want to consider a small personal loan through your bank. Some people start businesses using credit cards, but beware as they have the highest interest costs, making it even more difficult to fund your business long-term as interest eats up any profits.

Friends and Family: You may be able to approach family members or friends for cash as early investors. If you do know someone interested you may be able to get money interest free or at a very low interest rate.

- *Banks and Credit Unions:* You will need a well thought-out business plan to have a chance of getting a loan through a bank or credit union, and even then, given the current economic conditions, it's unlikely you'll secure one. You have a slightly better chance if you focus on securing a Small Business Administration loan through a participating bank, but if you are considered, expect a complex and long application process. You can find out more about SBA financing at *www.sba.gov/services/financialassistance/sbaloantopics.*
- *Venture Capital Firms:* Venture capitalists won't even look at your business unless you've already proved it to be successful and are looking for an investor to expand and get to the next level of operations.

Where to Work?

Where you want to start your business can be a key decision that ultimately determines your success or failure. That decision will drive your budgets and your method of operations. While working from home is by far the cheapest way to go it might not make sense if you're thinking of starting a retail business.

Many communities have limitations on what type of business you can run from your home. Most limit traffic into and out of the home for business purposes. So, if your business requires frequent visits from your customers, you should definitely check on the rules for running a business out of your home before you get started.

Buying an Existing Business

Starting a small business from home can help you bring in some quick cash after you've been laid off, but if you truly need a significant cash flow from your business to pay your mortgage and other major bills, you're probably better off buying a business that is already successful. Building a business that will provide significant cash flow can take ten to fifteen years or more, so you can't really count on a new business for cash flow to meet significant personal needs in the early years of operation.

Buying a business that already has proven profits and cash flow is a much better bet if you have the cash or can put together the funding. By buying a business you can also reduce the start-up costs of time, money, and energy.

Your cash flow from the business can start immediately because you'll have inventory and your location is established. You can count on an existing customer base and will have an easier time raising the additional capital you may need because you have a proven cash flow from the business.

But remember buying an existing business will require an initial investment that is much greater than starting a business from scratch. While it's great to have all the business basics in place—cash flow, customers, and inventory—you do have to pay for it all.

What to Buy?

That's the million-dollar question. You must decide on the type of business you want to buy. Don't look at something you don't enjoy doing. For example, you could find out about a great deal on a clothing store, but if you don't know anything about fashion, it's not the right choice for you.

Your best bet is to buy a business related to a field in which you've worked before. You also may want to think about buying a business related to your favorite hobby or some other passion. In fact, if you've been working part-time for a small business while you look for a full-time job, and you know it's doing well, you might find out if that business is for sale. Owners will rarely let employees know that a business is on the market, so it can't hurt to ask.

Finding Available Businesses

You may see a sign posted on a small business indicating it's for sale, but that's not usually the way it is done. More often than not you'll never know that a business you walk into every day is for sale. There are six ways to find available businesses:

1. *Newspaper Ads.* Check your local business newspapers for a listing of businesses for sale, but don't count on this as your primary source for finding opportunities. Very few businesses will advertise publicly that they are for sale.

2. *Business Professionals.* Check with bankers, lawyers, accountants, insurance agents, and real estate brokers you know for possible opportunities. Since they serve as advisors to small businesses, often they are the first to hear that a business may be on the market. If you don't know anyone in this network of professionals, call friends who you think may be connected.

3. *Business Suppliers.* Check with suppliers within the type of business you'd like to buy. They often know who might be thinking of selling their business. For example, if you'd like to own a bakery, check with suppliers that sell flour and other supplies to bakeries.

4. *Trade Associations.* Contact trade associations related to the type of business you want to buy. For example, if you want to buy a clothing store, find out if there is a local association for clothing retailers. Often employees of the association will be aware if one of their members wants to sell.

5. *Approach Owners Directly.* You can always approach an owner of a business you frequent and ask if they are thinking of selling. You never know if a person is thinking of retiring or moving and just hasn't taken any action yet. Yes, it's probably a long shot, but it's worth a try if you really like the business and see that it gets a steady stream of customers.

6. *Business Brokers.* Business brokers should be your last resort. These are people who earn commissions from the business owners who want to sell their business. They represent the interests of the person selling a business because that's who pays them. They only make money when they successfully sell that business, so you can't depend on them for quality advice.

If you do decide to work with a business broker, don't depend on them to help you through the process of due diligence. That's a process where you scour the business and its financial statements to determine if it's a good buy. Instead hire your own accountant and attorney to look over the deal.

You also may want to hire a business appraiser who can value the business for you. You can find out more about business value appraisers and what they offer you at the website of the American Society of Appraisers (*www.bvappraisers.org*).

Valuing the Business

Determining the value of a business can be very difficult. You'll find it easy to set a cash value for the things you can touch—inventory, store fixtures, equipment, and other tangible assets, but it's much harder to put a value on intangible things (things you can't touch), such as customer base and location.

As the new owner, you do have a customer base from which to build your business, but remember most small businesses are successful because of the owner—her relationship to customers, her vision, or her management skills and other unique talents. This can be very difficult to duplicate.

Many times when a business changes hands, old customers disappear. To try to minimize that loss you may be able to put a clause in the purchase contract that the selling owner must be involved with the business during the first year that you operate that business. You should clearly spell out the specifics of that involvement. That's not unusual and many small business owners see their business as their child and want it to succeed even after they are gone.

Letter of Intent to Purchase

If you decide that you've found your dream business, but you want time to investigate more deeply, you can sign a "Letter of Intent to Purchase." This will gain you some time to do further investigation, but secure your rights to buy the business. You should use this time to involve professionals you trust, such as your lawyer, accountant, or business advisor.

You will need to give the seller an earnest money deposit to show the seriousness of your intent, but since final purchase details have not been worked out, you should have the right to a full refund. When you do get to the point of actually offering a sales agreement to buy the business, this will be the key document that protects your rights. You will likely go through several drafts of the agreement with each draft being reviewed by your attorney and the seller's attorney.

Don't get impatient with what might seem like a tedious process. While you may be excited that you finally found just the right business, you don't want to rush this most crucial step and end up with problems later. When you're trying to evaluate the health of the business you're thinking of buying, as well as its future potential, you should ask to see certain records.

Due Diligence: Financial Statements

Few small businesses actually do financial statements consistently and some may never have done one at all. The business owner may need to generate them for you based on historical financial records from the past five years. It can sometimes take a long time to get these numbers.

When you get them, don't just read them and accept them. You need to observe the business operations and determine whether or not you think the numbers are realistic based on what you are seeing. For example, if the owner indicates that he has a $500,000 sales volume per month, but you can't figure out how he reaches that number based on the number of sales you see in a day, ask a lot of questions.

Five Years of Tax Returns

Compare the information on the financial statements you get with what the owner actually reported to the IRS. While it's not surprising if the owner shows you profit figures that are much higher than what he reports to the IRS, be sure you understand the differences and how he got to those lower profit figures he reported to the IRS. You may find that what he reports to the IRS is actually more truthful than what he gave you in financial statements as you dig into the figures.

Loan Documents

Sometimes you may plan to assume existing loans. If that's true, be sure you understand the terms and what your repayment obligations will be under the loan agreements. Although unlikely, if you think you can lower the interest rates by getting a larger loan from the Small Business Administration, you may want to add the pay off of any existing loans to your loan application.

Leases and Building Ownership

Review any lease agreements or ownership documents to find out what your obligations and rights will be under those leases or deeds. For example, you may find the lease for the store location runs out in a year. If that location is important to you and the success of maintaining the business, you could lose the location and the value you're paying for the business should be much lower.

Find out if you can extend that lease prior to signing the deal. When you talk to the property owner, he could tell you that he intends to increase the monthly rent obligation beyond what you consider feasible to keep the business financially viable. You could be forced to move the business soon after buying it, which can be the kiss of death to any business. Therefore, the location, which may have looked great to you, actually has little value.

Patents, Trademarks, and Copyrights

These intangible assets can be very important to the exclusivity of the business you plan to buy. Be certain the owner intends to sign these rights over to you. Also find out if any of them are running out soon.

For example, suppose a business you're thinking of buying owns a patent for its key product, which protects it from competition. This patent can be very valuable and make the business more expensive to buy. It likely also is critical to the business's continued success.

As you research the patent, you find out that the patent runs out in a year or two and you could lose your exclusive rights to the product. That makes the patent almost worthless. You'll likely see aggressive competition for your business fairly quickly after the patent runs out.

You also want to be sure that the owner plans to sign over the rights to the continuing use of any trademarks or product names that are unique to the business. You should have your attorney do a search for any conflicting trademarks or names and find out what has been registered. You certainly don't want to buy a store because of its name just to find out you have to change it in the future. You also want to protect yourself from the owner using the name you just bought to open a competing business.

Legal Problems

Ask to see information about any pending legal actions against the business. You could find out that there are pending lawsuits, administrative proceedings with governmental agencies, or claims that have been filed against the business.

Ask your attorney to review the information and figure out your potential liability. Be sure your purchase contract clearly spells out who will be responsible for what regarding any pending legal actions.

Accounting Reports

Ask to see all reports from the business's accountant. There are three types of reports that a Certified Public Accountant can provide—compilation, reviews, and audits. Here are what each involves:

1. *Compiled:* When an accountant signs off on a compilation report, he's merely giving you an organized look at the business's finances by preparing a professional presentation of the financial statements. The accountant has not reviewed or audited the owner's figures.

2. *Reviewed:* This type of report goes one step further. The accountant questions the employees and the owner about the numbers. While the accountant does not do a full audit, he can certify that he is not aware of any material modifications that are necessary for the information to conform to generally accepted accounting principles.

3. *Audited:* These are the most authentic types of audit reports. In this case, the accountant actually examines the numbers by going to the business and verifying the accuracy of the numbers for himself. While an auditor will not actually open every record or count each piece of inventory, he will do a series of tests on parts of the financial records to affirm they are accurate.

For example, he may review 10 to 20 percent of the customer records to see if they accurately reflect the numbers presented in accounts receivable. If he doesn't find any problems with his tests, he will sign a statement saying that the financial statements are accurate and do conform to generally accepted accounting principles.

While there is no doubt that audited financial statements are your best bet, few small business owners actually pay for them to be done.

In addition to requesting financial statements, you should also ask to see a list of all assets and a schedule of depreciation for those assets. Depreciation schedules can give you a good idea of the age of the assets and how long they may still be useful to the business.

If you find that most of the assets are fully depreciated or nearly fully depreciated, you need to plan to spend a lot of money on replacing those assets or repairing them. Newer assets with a significant value left will not need as much repair or replacement and your operating costs will be significantly lower.

Title and Title Insurance

If the business owns any property be sure to review the title and title insurance policy. Ask your attorney to check the title for any encumbrances, such as a lien against the title for past unpaid vendor bills. You also want to check any ownership documents for vehicles or other major equipment owned by the company that is being transferred to the new owner. Liens can also be taken against major assets, so you want to be sure your attorney checks for liens against vehicles or major equipment.

Workers' Compensation and Unemployment Claims

You should check with the workers' compensation insurance carrier to find out the claims history for the company and its current insurance rates. If there have been a number of claims filed, this could indicate a major problem with the business. You also should be aware that your future insurance rates could go up dramatically.

The same is true about unemployment claims. If the business owner frequently laid off people and has a significant claims history with the state unemployment office, you will find your payroll taxes will be higher than other similar businesses, which can be a drain on future profits.

Employee Benefits

Review benefits currently being offered to employees. You won't be able to cut them back easily if that's one way you plan to make the business more profitable. You will have a morale problem and could lose your employees.

Trade Secrets

You may not find that the small business you're considering has many trade secrets. The most valuable secret could be its customer lists. These lists could represent valuable assets, so be sure you protect them in your contract to buy the business. Find out who has copies of these lists and make sure they are protected by confidentiality agreements.

Zoning

Ask your lawyer to review any special zoning arrangements that might be in place. For example, if the current owner is operating under a temporary zoning variance or conditional use permit, it may not transfer to the new owner. You may have to seek a similar variance, which you might not get, or you could be severely limited with what you can do on the property. You may have some great ideas on how to expand the business or attract new customers, but your conditional use permit may not allow you to do what you plan.

Toxic Waste

If the business you are buying involves the disposal of toxic wastes, review the records detailing how toxic waste has been handled in the past. You certainly don't want to be stuck with the costs of cleaning up someone else's negligence.

Talk with Customers and Neighbors

After all the legal and financial information is gathered you still have some important detective work to do. Talk with the company's neighbors, vendors, employees, and customers. Find out what type of reputation the business has and how well it treats its customers.

If the business has a good reputation with its customers and neighbors, you'll have a much better chance of success than if it has a bad reputation. While you can post signs indicating the business has changed hands, if you are starting with a bad reputation you'll have to work twice as hard to rebuild the business. The business certainly isn't worth much beyond its hard assets if it has a bad reputation.

As you talk with suppliers, former employees, and others listen carefully for clues. They may be reluctant to talk for fear of reprisal. You probably won't get a straight answer if there are problems, but you might be able to tell by the tone of a person's voice or by a clear sign of evasiveness that there is a problem.

Buying a Franchise

Franchises are like buying a business in a box. You get all the basics of how to set up your business and how to sell the product. The information you get is based on lessons learned while the franchisor developed and ran his business.

Franchises can be a great alternative to starting your own business, especially if you don't have a lot of business or management experience, but don't expect to make much money in the first few years while you build your business and do expect to work long hours. Well-known franchises will help you attract customers, but buying a franchise is more like starting a new business than buying an existing business.

What is Franchising?

When you buy a franchise, you're actually buying a business relationship between yourself and the company that distributes a product or service nationwide. You buy a limited license from the company for the right to sell or distribute the product or service within a given area. There are two types of franchises—business-format and product-distribution.

1. *Business-Format Franchises:* These are more common today, and involve an agreement where you not only get the right to sell the product or service, but you also get an entire system for running your franchise. You get the right to operate your business under the national brand name. Dunkin' Donuts or Domino's Pizza are examples of this type of franchise.
2. *Product-Distribution Franchises:* These involve an agreement between you and the manufacturer. You are granted the rights to sell the manufacturer's product, but cannot operate under the manufacturer's name. Car dealerships are an example of this type of franchise.

The person or company who sells the rights to you is called the franchisor and you become the franchisee when you sign on the dotted line and buy the franchise.

Business-Format Franchise

Since business-format franchises have become so popular today you'll find lots of government regulation to give franchisees some protections. The Federal Trade Commission requires that three key elements must exist in a franchise business relationship:

1. You must be granted limited rights to use the company's trade name, service mark, logo, or other advertising symbol.
2. You must get the rights to use systems or methods associated with operating the core business.
3. You must pay the franchisor something in return for being granted these two rights.

You can find out more about the FTC rules and recommendations before buying a franchise at *www.ftc.gov/bcp/edu/pubs/consumer/invest/inv07.htm*. Be sure you read these rules before you sign any contracts.

A franchisor should give you training, marketing materials, and operating systems. Make sure you know what type of support you'll get before you sign any contracts. You should also get a manual that spells out how to operate your business. A good franchise package will include extensive management systems to help make your business a success.

Don't be naïve. You're not getting all this solely to help you succeed. The franchisor wants all his franchisees to run the business in exactly the same way with the same quality of products and services. If you don't run the business according to his systems, your business will not match the other franchisees.

That's a big problem for the national brand and company image. Customers of a particular franchise brand expect products or services worldwide to be the same no matter where they walk into the franchise.

Wouldn't you be disappointed if you walked into a Wendy's and ordered one of its old-fashioned hamburgers and it didn't taste like the hamburger you were expecting? You may think the new version is better than Wendy's burgers and would be pleasantly surprised, but if you were a Wendy's fan you'd probably complain to the company.

When you walk into 7-11, a McDonald's, or a Blimpie's or whatever franchise restaurant or store you visit regularly, you know what you want and expect to get it. The franchisor wants to be sure you do. That's why a good franchisor gives extensive training and support to all his franchisees.

You should get lots of advantages if you decide to buy into a franchise system:

National advertising to help drive customers to your business. If you're considering a franchise, but don't believe the company advertises its products, you need to ask the franchisor a lot of questions about how he plans to help you promote your business. Get those promises in writing.

Access to the purchasing power of a large, national operation. This should enable you to buy needed supplies at a lower price.

Tried-and-true marketing techniques. You can take advantage of what has worked for others in the franchise before, so you don't have to reinvent the wheel to get your business going.

Operational systems. This includes tools, controls, and procedures to help make your business successful.

National brand awareness. You can take advantage of the brand awareness that already exists for the product or service you want to sell.

Product-Distribution Franchise

If you're buying a product-distribution franchise then the rules are different. You'll find these types of arrangements most commonly when setting up a franchise in the automobile or oil industry.

For example, I'm sure you've noticed that most car dealerships open under the name of the person who owns the franchise or some other name he chooses, such as Don's Toyota or Jack's Chevy's. The franchise owner has the right to sell the specific brand of car, but does not get an entire package to run the business. He cannot name his car dealership General Motors or Ford Dealership. These corporations don't want to give the customer the impression it's a corporate owned business.

I won't discuss this type of franchise further because in most cases you must have millions to buy a distributorship and get involved in product-distribution franchising. You'll find that most of these types of franchises are sold to people who are already running one for the manufacturer. For example, a Toyota dealer might decide to buy the rights to open a Chevy dealership from General Motors.

Other common product-distribution dealerships include gas stations for the major oil companies or bottling distributorships for the major soda manufacturers. If you are interested in this type of franchise, then you'll definitely need to do a lot of additional research before pursuing this option.

Locating Your Franchise Opportunity

You've probably heard of the major franchises, such as UPS Stores, Wendy's, or McDonald's, but there's a lot more out there. In fact, franchises are available in more than 200 industry categories. The primary professional association within the franchise industry is called the International Franchise Association (IFA), which groups franchises in eighteen main categories. These categories include: automotive, fast food, baked goods, building and construction, business services, children-related businesses, education-related businesses, health care, lodging, maintenance services, personnel services, printing, real estate, restaurants, retail, service business, sports and recreation, and travel. You can find more details about the industries at the IFA website, *www.franchise.org*.

You might be most aware of fast-food franchises, but that may not be the best opportunity for you. You should only consider a restaurant business if you've run a restaurant before; otherwise you're sure to fail. Research what opportunities are available and find one that best matches your interests and experiences.

The IFA is a good place to start your research about franchising in general, as well as a good source for franchise opportunities. It's the world's largest clearinghouse on franchises. If the franchise you're considering is not a member of the IFA, tread very carefully.

Researching and finding the right franchise can take a lot of time. You can shortcut that a bit by working with a business broker. But be aware that business brokers are primarily interested in earning their commission and may not always put your interest first. The good news is that the broker is paid by the franchisor, so it won't be an out-of-pocket cost for you.

Here are three franchise business brokers you may want to contact for help in finding the right opportunity:

- FranChoice (*www.franchoice.com*). This is the broker recommended by the IFA.
- FranNet (*www.frannet.com*). FranNet is the world's largest network of franchise consultants. They help you learn about your choices and find the right one for you. Fran-

Net has fifty offices that are individually owned and operated.

- Entrepreneur Source (*www.theesource.com*). Entrepreneur Source focuses on consulting and training to help you succeed in your own business. They start with interviews and assessments to help you understand your goals, needs, and expectations, to be able to find options best suited for you.

If you know exactly which company you want to work with, go to their website for details. You don't have to use a broker to find a franchise. But you do need an attorney who understands franchise law and can advise you throughout the process.

Understanding Franchise Agreements

Once you pick your franchise, you'll then need to sign a franchise agreement that spells out what you are buying. You could be buying just one franchise store or you may want the right to build several store locations.

Another thing to consider is location. You may want to buy the rights to own and run all the stores within a particular geographic area, but unless you plan to work more hours than a full-time job requires, you don't want to bite off more than you can chew.

Contracts are set up in three different structures—single-unit franchises, multiple single-unit franchises, and area-development franchises. (Another structure—master franchises—is something not usually found in the United States.) Each of these structures involves a different type of agreement. Here are the basics of each type of structure:

Single-Unit Franchise. If you just want to own and operate one store or franchise unit, then you would sign an agreement for a single-unit franchise. This is the simplest form of franchise ownership. For some types of franchises, you don't even have to be thinking of operating out of a store front. You can do it from your home. For example, service franchises, such as carpet-cleaning franchises or house-cleaning franchises frequently are operated out of the franchisee's home. Customers find you through advertising online, in the phone book, local newspapers or community newsletters, on bulletin boards, or even by radio, depending on how you decide to advertise your business.

Multiple Single-Unit Franchises. If you're successful and the franchise bug bites, you may want to buy more than one franchise unit from the same franchisor. It's not unusual for a franchisee whose first unit proves profitable to sign a second agreement with the same franchisor for another location. This would be called a multiple single-unit franchise agreement. Since you're already familiar with the operation and the people involved, you can get that second or maybe third unit up and running much more quickly. Both you and the franchisor benefit from quicker start-up with fewer initial costs and less time for training.

Area-Development Franchises. If you're really successful and want to build more than one unit at a time, you might think about an area-development franchise. This gives you the right to run all franchises in a particular geographic area. This way, you can protect yourself from someone invading your territory. With this type of agreement, you would need to sign both an area-development franchise agreement, as well as single-unit development agreements for each franchise you open. The area-development agreement specifies development rights, but the unit-development agreement governs the terms for how each unit will be run and the franchise fees for the unit.

If you decide franchising is for you, be sure to have an attorney who is familiar with franchise law review your contract. All offers to buy a franchise must comply with standards outlined by the Federal Trade Commission (FTC) for a Uniform Franchise Offering Circular (UFOC), but even under the rules of the UFOC there are different types of franchise agreements you can be offered. If you want more detail, download the FTC's "A Consumer Guide to Buying a Franchise" (*www .pueblo.gsa.gov/cic_text/smbuss/franchise/franchise.pdf*).

How Much Cash Do You Need?

You can find franchise opportunities that will let you get started with just $20,000 to $30,000, but they won't be well-known names. If you want to buy into a well-established franchise, you'll probably need to front at least $100,000 in cash.

RECAP: It should take well more than one week to complete the tasks in this chapter. But that's expected as you're now starting something that you'll be running for the foreseeable future. Take the time to build the proper foundation for your business by following these steps:

- Take small business courses online to learn the basics and nuances of developing and running your own business.
- Start or buy a business in a field you already know. Don't try to start or buy a business just because it seems like a good opportunity.
- Ask yourself the tough question about why someone would want to buy from you and take the time to write down the answer.
- Know the pros and cons of starting a new business, buying an established business, and buying a franchise. Decide which fits your knowledge base and time frame.

Conclusion

GETTING UP, DUSTING off your clothes, and restarting your life after a layoff is hard work—but it's also a great opportunity to reinvent yourself into just what you want to be. Instead of getting depressed about your job loss, think of this as the perfect time to revisit your life and focus on what you've always wanted to do.

Most of us went from high school to work, or from high school to the military to work, or from high school to college to work. We made career decisions with little experience of the realities of the working world. We chose jobs based on what we wanted to do as teenagers.

Now is the time to think about whether that's still what you want to do today. You may discover that your career choice isn't a good fit and you want to explore other options. Take advantage of services offered by your state, such as career counseling and retraining, to find and prepare for your true calling.

Your layoff can be just what you need to restart your life, but you'll need to do a lot of soul searching to ensure you're headed in the right direction. Hopefully this book has given you lots of fodder to consider how you may want to stage your reinvention!

Building for Long-Term Financial Security

Of course, the key lies in finding something that will provide financial security. The idea of long-term job security is not plausible in today's economic climate. Companies today are beholden to stockholders and thus forced to focus on the bottom line. The days when corporations worried about their image or employee morale before they laid off staff are long since past.

If you do land a position with a great, stable company stay there as long as you enjoy the work. But keep in mind that the only true guarantee to avoid a layoff is to start your own business. I did that eight years ago and I now know I can never be laid off. My income may be unsteady, but I'm the one who controls that by how aggressively I promote myself to find contract opportunities. It works for me because I am no longer worrying about when the axe may fall unexpectedly.

Planning for Tomorrow

You need to keep your eyes focused on the future. Don't wait around for your company to come up with just the right promotion. Always be looking at your next steps. Always be building your networks and maintaining contact with the members of your network. Remember: Networks are about sharing, so look for ways you can help the members of your network, don't just look for what your network can do for you.

If you dream of starting a business, start working on it today. I worked a full-time job for almost four years before I took the leap. I invested time planning out what I wanted to do and worked on saving the money I'd need for at least a year so I'd be able to support myself while I built my business. A layoff disrupted my plans and I only had six months saved, but

I decided to take the leap anyway. I've never regretted that decision.

The Road Back to Happiness

Your road back to happiness after a layoff is totally in your own hands. Don't count on anyone to pave that road for you. While family and friends may offer invaluable support and help, the only one that can truly get you back on that road is yourself. You're the only one who knows what will make you happy.

Once you know what that is, don't hesitate to seek help to get there! You may need to go back to school or you may need to move. These types of decisions you can't make without talking with your family members as you need them to support your choices. Don't fool yourself—making a major change to get back on the road to happiness will require a lot of support; I don't recommend you go it alone. But in the end, I think you'll find it was worth it.

Good luck with your search, and I hope to meet you on the road to happiness one day.

Resources

Websites

Researching Companies

www.sec.gov—U.S. Securities and Exchange Commission official site

www.finance.yahoo.com—Yahoo site that includes news and information on businesses

www.hoovers.com—includes information on industries and companies as well as contacts and expert advice

www.vault.com—information on companies and industries, along with sample resumes and other job-hunting tips

www.wetfeet.com—a good career site, especially for younger workers

Discrimination

www.eeoc.gov—official site of the U.S. Equal Employment Opportunity Commission

Insurance

www.medhealthinsurance.com—tips and information on medical insurance, both for the employed and unemployed

Credit and Mortgage Problems

www.bankrate.com—information on banks, mortgage and interest rates, and general credit questions *www.hud.gov/foreclosure/index.cfm*—site of the U.S. Department of Housing and Urban Development, dealing with foreclosures

www.nfcc.org—site of the National Foundation for Credit Counseling

www.transunion.com—credit reporting bureau

www.equifax.com—credit reporting bureau

www.experian.com—credit reporting bureau

Job Searching

The following sites contain tips on job searching, sample resumes, suggestions on salary and benefit negotiation, and further resources to help in your job search.

www.careeronestop.com

www.careerbuilder.com

www.google.com/Top/Business/Employment/Job_Search

The following are two of the most important job sites on the web, containing thousands of jobs sorted by profession.

www.monster.com

www.hotjobs.yahoo.com

Career Planning

www.nbcc.org/counselorfind2—site of the National Board of Certified Counselors, helpful for finding job counseling

www.morris.umn.edu/services/career/career_planning/valquestion.php—contains a useful Values Questionnaire to figure out your career and life goals

www.career-intelligence.com/assessment/career_values.html—includes exercises for figuring out your values and how they integrate with your job goals

http://cehd.umn.edu/ETCS/career/ValuesSelfAssessment.pdf—a work-related values assessment, originally published by the U.S. Department of Labor

www.pearsonassessments.com/tests/ciss.htm—Pearson skills assessment test, useful in determining job goals

www.self-directed-search.com—Dr. John L. Holland's test for determining your career goals and skills

www.career-intelligence.com—a site of career advice for working women

www.advisorteam.com/temperament_sorter—includes a Temperament Sorter Test, helpful in determining job goals

www.lifeworktransitions.com/exercises/exercs.html—contains tips and exercises for career transitions, including layoffs

Networking

www.linkedin.com—the most important professional networking site

http://en.wikipedia.org/wili/List_of_social_networking_website—contains a comprehensive list of social-networking sites.

www.classmates.com—social-networking site for former high-school and college classmates

Self Employment

www.irs.gov/pub/irs-pdf/fss8.pdf—Internal Revenue Service form to determine your status as a contractor

www.sba.gov—official site of the Small Business Administration

www.score.org—small business development site, containing tips and development tools for small businesses

www.theesource.com—site of the Entrepreneur's Source, containing advice and information relevant to small businesses

www.pueblo.gsa.gov/cic_text/smbuss/franchise/franchise.pdf—advice from the Federal Trade Commission about buying a franchise

Books

Knock 'em Dead: The Ultimate Job Search Guide. Martin Yate. Adams Media, 2008.

What Color is Your Parachute? A Practical Manual for Job-Hunters and Career Changers. Richard Nelson Bolles. Ten Speed Press, 2008.

Fired, Laid Off or Forced Out! Richard Busse. Sphinx Publishing, 2005.

Career Comeback: Eight steps to Getting Back on Your Feet When You're Fired, Laid Off, or Your Business Venture Has Failed— And Finding More Job Satisfaction Than Ever Before. Bradley Richardson. Broadway, 2004.

Landing on the Right Side of Your Ass: A Survival Guide for the Recently Unemployed. Michael Laskoff. Three Rivers Press, 2004.

We Got Fired!: . . . And It's the Best Thing That Ever Happened to Us. Harvey MacKay. Ballantine, 2004.

Index

Index

About the Author

Lita Epstein, MBA, has written more than a dozen business books on topics ranging from retirement planning to social security and Medicare. She is also the author of *Streetwise Crash Course MBA* and *Streetwise Retirement Planning*. She is a faculty member of the College of Graduate Business and Management at the University of Phoenix.